the Responsibilities *of* Wealth

Philanthropic Studies
Robert L. Payton and Dwight F. Burlingame, general editors

indiana
university
press
BLOOMINGTON AND INDIANAPOLIS

the Responsibilities *of* Wealth

EDITED BY DWIGHT F. BURLINGAME

The paper used in this publication meets the minimum requirements of American
National Standard for Information Sciences—Permanence of Paper for Printed
Library Materials, ANSI Z39.48-1984.

♾ ™

Manufactured in the United States of America

Library of Congress Cataloging-in-Publication Data

The Responsibilities of wealth / edited by Dwight Burlingame.
    p.   cm. — (Philanthropic studies)
  Includes index.
  ISBN 0-253-31279-5 (alk. paper)
  1. Wealth—Moral and ethical aspects. 2. Humanitarianism.
3. Endowments. 4. Social service. I. Burlingame, Dwight.
II. Series.
HC79.W4R47 1992
330.1′6—dc20   91-17000

1 2 3 4 5 96 95 94 93 92

contents

preface

One can hardly read a newspaper, listen to a radio, or watch television without encountering some reference to money and wealth. Facing the question of the responsibility of wealth is not required of most of us, and certainly is not high on the list of scholarly inquiry. However, it is an important question especially as we address the broader issue of understanding the historical context of philanthropy in our society.

It is hoped that this volume may make a contribution to the field and will encourage others to apply more sustained inquiries into the subject, since the values of a society are often reflected in what it chooses to support—voluntarily and politically.

The title of this book was inspired by the theme of the Second Annual Symposium of the Indiana University Center on Philanthropy, held in 1988. It assumes that the wealthy are in some way obliged to be philanthropic. Andrew Carnegie in "The Gospel of Wealth" attempted to convince his wealthy peers of this point of view. His essay could be profitably read by many wealthy today if current estimates that only half of all U.S. millionaires are charitably-minded are true. The point is not whether we agree or disagree with Carnegie's particular opinions; it is that we should contemplate and reflect on a capitalistic society's responsibility in the use of its wealth for the public good. This volume opens with a reprint of his "Gospel," setting the stage for the other authors in this volume to reflect on this important and often neglected topic.

Carnegie's reflection on socially responsible wealth a hundred years ago was of course not new. The idea certainly flourished in Europe in the fifteenth and sixteenth centuries and reached new development as it was practiced by Carnegie and the Rockefellers in late nineteenth century America. The new industrial elites did not practice a disinterested "altruism" but rather a form of "enlightened self-interest." Carnegie in particular was searching for ways in which he could distribute his wealth which would not have "a degrading, pauperizing tendency upon its recipients" but which would help them help themselves.

In recent years, Barry Karl has emerged as one of philanthropy's leading historians. His suggested retitling of Carnegie's essay to "The Gospel of Wealth and Poverty" helps us begin to understand the complex relationship between wealth and poverty and thus gain a greater appreciation of the thinking of Carnegie and his contemporaries on why scientific philanthropy was different from charity; i.e., that philanthropy accepted the responsibility to change the conditions that caused poverty. In his essay Karl illustrates quite persuasively that part of Carnegie and Rockefeller's failure to engage in public welfare support was based upon their belief that no one industry or individual could be the welfare net, and thus a larger system needed to be provided.

Albert Anderson examines Aristotle's writings to find a profound and complex perception of responsibility and in turn what it means to be philanthropic. By distributing one's wealth well, by directing it to the public good and seeking no favors in turn, can one be said to be philanthropic?

Jonathan Riley raises the question: Why does morality apparently prescribe active giving by the wealthy themselves rather than simply mandating government redistribution through progressive taxation? Carnegie found his answer in part in the argument that liberal government is limited to provision of those public goods that all citizens need and is not able to discriminate as philanthropy must. Riley provides an insight into how we might develop and encourage through legal means the revival of liberal philanthropy in America.

Kenneth Fox traces corporate philanthropy through business history and concludes that the notion of "corporate social responsibility" sets a higher level of behavior which most business managers did not wish to carry out. In essence, business philanthropy through corporate giving has failed to carry out Carnegie's creed that the creators of society's wealth are the proper leaders of its philanthropy.

Louise W. Knight offers in her essay a contrasting view of the responsibility of wealth by one of Carnegie's contemporaries, Jane Addams. Jane Addams's views were based on the Judeo-Christian tenet that everyone deserves equal respect; therefore, she promoted social justice through interaction with the poor—most notably through Hull House.

The work concludes with a chapter devoted to how religion addresses the issue of responsibility of wealth. Robert L. Payton argues that the philanthropic tradition is based upon religious traditions and thus to create more effective and more responsible philanthropy we need to study the connections between religion and philanthropy.

After reading the essays in this volume, one is inspired to reflect on the responsibilities of wealth, guided vicariously by civic responsibility, enlightened self-interest, and religious conviction. Upon his retirement Harry Oppenheimer, former chairman of Anglo-American in South Africa, said in his farewell speech: "We have to believe, and by our practices demonstrate, that the pursuit of business efficiency and the search for a free and just society are not contradictory objectives, but in fact two aspects of the same thing—two sides of the same coin."[1] How similar this is to Carnegie's statement of the problem some one hundred years earlier: "The problem of our age is the proper administration of wealth, that the ties of brotherhood may still bind together the rich and poor in harmonious relationship."

The third or independent sector must live in a political environment certainly different from and, I would argue, more intrusive than was the case a century and even fifty years ago. However, the growth of the American welfare state and government spending has not, contrary to popular belief, minimized the role of the voluntary sector. Only in the last two decades have we seen organized attention to the study of philanthropy—spearheaded by the independent sector—and academic centers such as those at Yale, New York University, Duke, San Francisco, and Indiana, to name a few. May the food for thought in this little volume contribute to greater dialogue among practitioners and scholars in the next decade.

Dwight F. Burlingame

Note

1. James A. Joseph, *The Charitable Impulse: Wealth and Social Conscience in Communities and Cultures Outside the United States* (New York: The Foundation Center, 1989), p. 50.

the Gospel _of_ Wealth

ANDREW CARNEGIE

I. The Problem of the Administration of Wealth

The problem of our age is the proper administration of wealth,
that the ties of brotherhood may still bind together the rich and
poor in harmonious relationship.[1] The conditions of human life
have not only been changed, but revolutionized, within the past
few hundred years. In former days there was little difference between the dwelling, dress, food, and environment of the chief and
those of his retainers. The Indians are to-day where civilzed man
then was. When visiting the Sioux, I was led to the wigwam of
the chief. It was like the others in external appearance, and even
within the difference was trifling between it and those of the poorest
of his braves. The contrast between the palace of the millionaire
and the cottage of the laborer with us to-day measures the change
which has come with civilization. This change, however, is not to
be deplored, but welcomed as highly beneficial. It is well, nay,
essential, for the progress of the race that the houses of some should
be homes for all that is highest and best in literature and the arts,
and for all the refinements of civilization, rather than that none
should be so. Much better this great irregularity than universal
squalor. Without wealth there can be no Mæcenas. The "good old
times" were not good old times. Neither master nor servant was
as well situated then as to-day. A relapse to old conditions would
be disastrous to both—not the least so to him who serves—and

Excerpted from _The Gospel of Wealth and Other Timely Essays_ by Andrew
Carnegie, ed. Edward C. Kirkland. Reprinted by permission of Harvard University
Press, publisher, ©1962 by the President and Fellows of Harvard College.

would sweep away civilization with it. But whether the change be for good or ill, it is upon us, beyond our power to alter, and, therefore, to be accepted and made the best of. It is a waste of time to criticize the inevitable.

It is easy to see how the change has come. One illustration will serve for almost every phase of the cause. In the manufacture of products we have the whole story. It applies to all combinations of human industry, as stimulated and enlarged by the inventions of this scientific age. Formerly, articles were manufactured at the domestic hearth, or in small shops which formed part of the household. The master and his apprentices worked side by side, the latter living with the master, and therefore subject to the same conditions. When these apprentices rose to be masters, there was little or no change in their mode of life, and they, in turn, educated succeeding apprentices in the same routine. There was, substantially, social equality, and even political equality, for those engaged in industrial pursuits had then little or no voice in the State.

The inevitable result of such a mode of manufacture was crude articles at high prices. To-day the world obtains commodities of excellent quality at prices which even the preceding generation would have deemed incredible. In the commercial world similar causes have produced similar results, and the race is benefited thereby. The poor enjoy what the rich could not before afford. What were the luxuries have become the necessaries of life. The laborer has now more comforts than the farmer had a few generations ago. The farmer has more luxuries than the landlord had, and is more richly clad and better housed. The landlord has books and pictures rarer and appointments more artistic than the king could then obtain.

The price we pay for this salutary change is, no doubt, great. We assemble thousands of operatives in the factory, and in the mine, of whom the employer can know little or nothing, and to whom he is little better than a myth. All intercourse between them is at an end. Rigid castes are formed, and, as usual, mutual ignorance breeds mutual distrust. Each caste is without sympathy with the other, and ready to credit anything disparaging in regard to it. Under the law of competition, the employer of thousands is forced into the strictest economies, among which the rates paid to labor figure prominently, and often there is friction between the employer and the employed, between capital and labor, between rich and poor. Human society loses homogeneity.

The price which society pays for the law of competition, like the price it pays for cheap comforts and luxuries, is also great; but the advantages of this law are also greater still than its cost—for it is to this law that we owe our wonderful material development, which brings improved conditions in its train. But, whether the law be benign or not, we must say of it, as we say of the change in the conditions of men to which we have referred: It is here; we cannot evade it; no substitutes for it have been found; and while the law may be sometimes hard for the individual, it is best for the race, because it insures the survival of the fittest in every department. We accept and welcome, therefore, as conditions to which we must accommodate ourselves, great inequality of environment; the concentration of business, industrial and commercial, in the hands of a few; and the law of competition between these, as being not only beneficial, but essential to the future progress of the race. Having accepted these, it follows that there must be great scope for the exercise of special ability in the merchant and in the manufacturer who has to conduct affairs upon a great scale. That this talent for organization and management is rare among men is proved by the fact that it invariably secures enormous rewards for its possessor, no matter where or under what laws or conditions. The experienced in affairs always rate the MAN whose services can be obtained as a partner as not only the first consideration, but such as render the question of his capital scarcely worth considering: for able men soon create capital; in the hands of those without the special talent required, capital soon takes wings. Such men become interested in firms or corporations using millions; and, estimating only simple interest to be made upon the capital invested, it is inevitable that their income must exceed their expenditure and that they must, therefore, accumulate wealth. Nor is there any middle ground which such men can occupy, because the great manufacturing or commercial concern which does not earn at least interest upon its capital soon becomes bankrupt. It must either go forward or fall behind; to stand still is impossible. It is a condition essential to its successful operation that it should be thus far profitable, and even that, in addition to interest on capital, it should make profit. It is a law, as certain as any of the others named, that men possessed of this peculiar talent for affairs, under the free play of economic forces must, of necessity, soon be in receipt of more revenue than can be judiciously expended upon themselves; and this law is as beneficial for the race as the others.

Objections to the foundations upon which society is based are not in order, because the condition of the race is better with these than it has been with any other which has been tried. Of the effect of any new substitutes proposed we cannot be sure. The Socialist or Anarchist who seeks to overturn present conditions is to be regarded as attacking the foundation upon which civilization itself rests, for civilization took its start from the day when the capable, industrious workman said to his incompetent and lazy fellow, "If thou dost not sow, thou shalt not reap," and thus ended primitive Communism by separating the drones from the bees. One who studies this subject will soon be brought face to face with the conclusion that upon the sacredness of property civilization itself depends—the right of the laborer to his hundred dollars in the savings-bank, and equally the legal right of the millionaire to his millions. Every man must be allowed "to sit under his own vine and fig-tree, with none to make afraid," if human society is to advance, or even to remain so far advanced as it is. To those who propose to substitute Communism for this intense Individualism, the answer therefore is: The race has tried that. All progress from that barbarous day to the present time has resulted from its displacement. Not evil, but good, has come to the race from the accumulation of wealth by those who have had the ability and energy to produce it. But even if we admit for a moment that it might be better for the race to discard its present foundation, Individualism,—that it is a nobler ideal that man should labor, not for himself alone, but in and for a brotherhood of his fellows, and share with them all in common, realizing Swedenborg's idea of heaven,[2] where, as he says, the angels derive their happiness, not from laboring for self, but for each other,—even admit all this, and a sufficient answer is, This is not evolution, but revolution. It necessitates the changing of human nature itself—a work of eons, even if it were good to change it, which we cannot know.

It is not practicable in our day or in our age. Even if desirable theoretically, it belongs to another and long-succeeding sociological stratum. Our duty is with what is practicable now—with the next step possible in our day and generation. It is criminal to waste our energies in endeavoring to uproot, when all we can profitably accomplish is to bend the universal tree of humanity a little in the direction most favorable to the production of good fruit under existing circumstances. We might as well urge the destruction of the highest existing type of man because he failed to reach our ideal as to favor the destruction of Individualism, Private Property, the Law of Accumulation of Wealth, and the Law of Competition; for these are the highest result of human experience, the soil in which society, so far, has produced the best fruit. Unequally or unjustly, perhaps, as these laws sometimes operate, and imperfect as they appear to the Idealist, they are, nevertheless, like the highest type of man, the best and most valuable of all that humanity has yet accomplished.

We start, then, with a condition of affairs under which the best interests of the race are promoted, but which inevitably gives wealth to the few. Thus far, accepting conditions as they exist, the situation can be surveyed and pronounced good. The question then arises,— and if the foregoing be correct, it is the only question with which we have to deal,—What is the proper mode of administering wealth after the laws upon which civilization is founded have thrown it into the hands of the few? And it is of this great question that I believe I offer the true solution. It will be understood that fortunes are here spoken of, not moderate sums saved by many years of effort, the returns from which are required for the comfortable maintenance and education of families. This is not wealth, but only competence, which it should be the aim of all to acquire, and which it is for the best interests of society should be acquired.

There are but three modes in which surplus wealth can be disposed of. It can be left to the families of the decedents; or it can be bequeathed for public purposes; or, finally, it can be administered by its possessors during their lives. Under the first and second modes most of the wealth of the world that has reached the few has hitherto been applied. Let us in turn consider each of these modes. The first is the most injudicious. In monarchical countries, the estates and the greatest portion of the wealth are left to the first son, that the vanity of the parent may be gratified by the thought that his name and title are to descend unimpaired to succeeding generations. The condition of this class in Europe to-day teaches the failure of such hopes or ambitions. The successors have become impoverished through their follies, or from the fall in the value of land. Even in Great Britain the strict law of entail has been found inadequate to maintain an hereditary class. Its soil is rapidly passing into the hands of the stranger. Under republican institutions the division of property among the children is much fairer; but the question which forces itself upon thoughtful men in all lands is, Why should men leave great fortunes to their children? If this is done from affection, is it not misguided affection? Observation teaches that, generally speaking, it is not well for the children that they should be so burdened. Neither is it well for the State. Beyond providing for the wife and daughters moderate sources of income, and very moderate allowances indeed, if any, for the sons, men may well hesitate; for it is no longer questionable that great sums bequeathed often work more for the injury than for the good of the recipients. Wise men will soon conclude that, for the best interests of the members of their families, and of the State, such bequests are an improper use of their means.

It is not suggested that men who have failed to educate their sons to earn a livelihood shall cast them adrift in poverty. If any man has seen fit to rear his sons with a view to their living idle lives, or, what is highly commendable, has instilled in them the sentiment that they are in a position to labor for public ends without reference to pecuniary considerations, then, of course, the duty of the parent is to see that such are provided for in moderation. There are instances of millionaires' sons unspoiled by wealth, who, being rich, still perform great services to the community. Such are the very salt of the earth, as valuable as, unfortunately, they are rare. It is not the exception, however, but the rule, that men must regard; and, looking at the usual result of enormous sums conferred upon legatees, the thoughtful man must shortly say, "I would as soon leave to my son a curse as the almighty dollar," and admit to himself that it is not the welfare of the children, but family pride, which inspires these legacies.

As to the second mode, that of leaving wealth at death for public uses, it may be said that this is only a means for the disposal of wealth, provided a man is content to wait until he is dead before he becomes of much good in the world. Knowledge of the results of legacies bequeathed is not calculated to inspire the brightest hopes of much posthumous good being accomplished by them. The cases are not few in which the real object sought by the testator is not attained, nor are they few in which his real wishes are thwarted. In many cases the bequests are so used as to become only monuments of his folly. It is well to remember that it requires the exercise of not less ability than that which acquires it, to use wealth so as to be really beneficial to the community. Besides this, it may fairly be said that no man is to be extolled for doing what he cannot help doing, nor is he to be thanked by the community to which he only leaves wealth at death. Men who leave vast sums in this way may fairly be thought men who would not have left it at all had they been able to take it with them. The memories of such cannot be held in grateful remembrance, for there is no grace in their gifts. It is not to be wondered at that such bequests seem so generally to lack the blessing.

The growing disposition to tax more and more heavily large estates left at death is a cheering indication of the growth of a salutary change in public opinion. The State of Pennsylvania now takes—subject to some exceptions—one tenth of the property left by its citizens. The budget presented in the British Parliament the other day proposes to increase the death duties; and, most significant of all, the new tax is to be a graduated one. Of all forms of taxation this seems the wisest.[3] Men who continue hoarding great sums all their lives, the proper use of which for public ends would work good to the community from which it chiefly came, should be made to feel that the community, in the form of the State, cannot thus be deprived of its proper share. By taxing estates heavily at death the State marks its condemnation of the selfish millionaire's unworthy life.

It is desirable that nations should go much further in this direction. Indeed, it is difficult to set bounds to the share of a rich man's estate which should go at his death to the public through the agency of the State, and by all means such taxes should be graduated, beginning at nothing upon moderate sums to dependents, and increasing rapidly as the amounts swell, until of the millionaire's hoard, as of Shylock's, at least

> The other half
> Comes to the privy coffer of the State.[4]

This policy would work powerfully to induce the rich man to attend to the administration of wealth during his life, which is the end that society should always have in view, as being by far the most fruitful for the people. Nor need it be feared that this policy would sap the root of enterprise and render men less anxious to accumulate, for, to the class whose ambition it is to leave great fortunes and to be talked about after their death, it will attract even more attention, and, indeed, be a somewhat nobler ambition, to have enormous sums paid over to the State from their fortunes.

There remains, then, only one mode of using great fortunes; but in this we have the true antidote for the temporary unequal distribution of wealth, the reconciliation of the rich and the poor— a reign of harmony, another ideal, differing, indeed, from that of the Communist in requiring only the further evolution of existing conditions, not the total overthrow of our civilization. It is founded upon the present most intense Individualism, and the race is prepared to put it in practice by degrees whenever it pleases. Under its sway we shall have an ideal State, in which the surplus wealth of the few will become, in the best sense, the property of the many, because administered for the common good; and this wealth, passing through the hands of the few, can be made a much more potent force for the elevation of our race than if distributed in small sums to the people themselves. Even the poorest can be made to see this, and to agree that great sums gathered by some of their fellow-citizens and spent for public purposes, from which the masses reap the principal benefit, are more valuable to them than if scattered among themselves in trifling amounts through the course of many years.

If we consider the results which flow from the Cooper Institute, for instance, to the best portion of the race in New York not possessed of means, and compare these with those which would have ensued for the good of the masses from an equal sum distributed by Mr. Cooper in his lifetime in the form of wages, which is the highest form of distribution, being for work done and not for charity, we can form some estimate of the possibilities for the improvement of the race which lie embedded in the present law of the accumulation of wealth. Much of this sum, if distributed in small quantities among the people, would have been wasted in the indulgence of appetite, some of it in excess, and it may be doubted whether even the part put to the best use, that of adding to the comforts of the home, would have yielded results for the race, as a race, at all comparable to those which are flowing and are to flow from the Cooper Institute from generation to generation.[5] Let the advocate of violent or radical change ponder well this thought.

We might even go so far as to take another instance—that of Mr. Tilden's bequest of five millions of dollars for a free library in the city of New York; but in referring to this one cannot help saying involuntarily: How much better if Mr. Tilden had devoted the last years of his own life to the proper administration of this immense sum; in which case neither legal contest nor any other cause of delay could have interfered with his aims. But let us assume that Mr. Tilden's millions finally become the means of giving to this city a noble public library, where the treasures of the world contained in books will be open to all forever, without money and without price.[6] Considering the good of that part of the race which congregates in and around Manhattan Island, would its permanent benefit have been better promoted had these millions been allowed to circulate in small sums through the hands of the masses? Even the most strenuous advocate of Communism must entertain a doubt upon this subject. Most of those who think will probably entertain no doubt whatever.

Poor and restricted are our opportunities in this life, narrow our horizon, our best work most imperfect; but rich men should be thankful for one inestimable boon. They have it in their power during their lives to busy themselves in organizing benefactions from which the masses of their fellows will derive lasting advantage, and thus dignify their own lives. The highest life is probably to be reached, not by such imitation of the life of Christ as Count Tolstoi gives us, but, while animated by Christ's spirit, by recognizing the changed conditions of this age, and adopting modes of expressing this spirit suitable to the changed conditions under which we live, still laboring for the good of our fellows, which was the essence of his life and teaching, but laboring in a different manner.

This, then, is held to be the duty of the man of wealth: To set an example of modest, unostentatious living, shunning display or extravagance; to provide moderately for the legitimate wants of those dependent upon him; and, after doing so, to consider all surplus revenues which come to him simply as trust funds, which he is called upon to administer, and strictly bound as a matter of duty to administer in the manner which, in his judgment, is best calculated to produce the most beneficial results for the community—the man of wealth thus becoming the mere trustee and agent for his poorer brethren, bringing to their service his superior wisdom, experience, and ability to administer, doing for them better than they would or could do for themselves.

We are met here with the difficulty of determining what are moderate sums to leave to members of the family; what is modest, unostentatious living; what is the test of extravagance. There must be different standards for different conditions. The answer is that it is as impossible to name exact amounts or actions as it is to define good manners, good taste, or the rules of propriety; but, nevertheless, these are verities, well known, although indefinable. Public sentiment is quick to know and to feel what offends these. So in the case of wealth. The rule in regard to good taste in dress of men or women applies here. Whatever makes one conspicuous offends the canon. If any family be chiefly known for display, for extravagance in home, table, or equipage, for enormous sums ostentatiously spent in any form upon itself—if these be its chief distinctions, we have no difficulty in estimating its nature or culture. So likewise in regard to the use or abuse of its surplus wealth, or to generous, free-handed cooperation in good public uses, or to unabated efforts to accumulate and hoard to the last, or whether they administer or bequeath. The verdict rests with the best and most enlightened public sentiment. The community will surely judge, and its judgments will not often be wrong.

The best uses to which surplus wealth can be put have already been indicated. Those who would administer wisely must, indeed, be wise; for one of the serious obstacles to the improvement of our race is indiscriminate charity. It were better for mankind that the millions of the rich were thrown into the sea than so spent as to encourage the slothful, the drunken, the unworthy. Of every thousand dollars spent in so-called charity to-day, it is probable that nine hundred and fifty dollars is unwisely spent—so spent, indeed, as to produce the very evils which it hopes to mitigate or cure. A well-known writer of philosophic books admitted the other day that he had given a quarter of a dollar to a man who approached him as he was coming to visit the house of his friend. He knew nothing of the habits of this beggar, knew not the use that would be made of this money, although he had every reason to suspect that it would be spent improperly. This man professed to be a disciple of Herbert Spencer; yet the quarter-dollar given that night will probably work more injury than all the money will do good which its thoughtless donor will ever be able to give in true charity. He only gratified his own feelings, saved himself from annoyance— and this was probably one of the most selfish and very worst actions of his life, for in all respects he is most worthy.

In bestowing charity, the main consideration should be to help those who will help themselves; to provide part of the means by which those who desire to improve may do so; to give those who desire to rise the aids by which they may rise; to assist, but rarely or never to do all. Neither the individual nor the race is improved by almsgiving. Those worthy of assistance, except in rare cases, seldom require assistance. The really valuable men of the race never do, except in case of accident or sudden change. Every one has, of course, cases of individuals brought to his own knowledge where temporary assistance can do genuine good, and these he will not overlook. But the amount which can be wisely given by the individual for individuals is necessarily limited by his lack of knowledge of the circumstances connected with each. He is the only true reformer who is as careful and as anxious not to aid the unworthy as he is to aid the worthy, and perhaps, even more so, for in almsgiving more injury is probably done by rewarding vice than by relieving virtue.

The rich man is thus almost restricted to following the examples of Peter Cooper, Enoch Pratt of Baltimore, Mr. Pratt of Brooklyn, Senator Stanford,[7] and others, who know that the best means of benefiting the community is to place within its reach the ladders upon which the aspiring can rise—free libraries, parks, and means of recreation, by which men are helped in body and mind; works of art, certain to give pleasure and improve the public taste; and public institutions of various kinds, which will improve the general condition of the people; in this manner returning their surplus wealth to the mass of their fellows in the forms best calculated to do them lasting good.

Thus is the problem of rich and poor to be solved. The laws of accumulation will be left free, the laws of distribution free. Indi-

vidualism will continue, but the millionaire will be but a trustee
for the poor, intrusted for a season with a great part of the increased
wealth of the community, but administering it for the community
far better than it could or would have done for itself. The best
minds will thus have reached a stage in the development of the
race in which it is clearly seen that there is no mode of disposing
of surplus wealth creditable to thoughtful and earnest men into
whose hands it flows, save by using it year by year for the general
good. This day already dawns. Men may die without incurring the
pity of their fellows, still sharers in great business enterprises from
which their capital cannot be or has not been withdrawn, and
which is left chiefly at death for public uses; yet the day is not far
distant when the man who dies leaving behind him millions of
available wealth, which was free to him to administer during life,
will pass away "unwept, unhonored, and unsung," no matter to
what uses he leaves the dross which he cannot take with him. Of
such as these the public verdict will then be: "The man who dies
thus rich dies disgraced."

Such, in my opinion is the true gospel concerning wealth, obedience to which is destined some day to solve the problem of the
rich and the poor, and to bring "Peace on earth, among men
good will."

II. The Best Fields for Philanthropy

While "The Gospel of Wealth" has met a cordial reception upon
this side of the Atlantic, it is natural that in the motherland it
should have attracted more attention, because the older civilization
is at present brought more clearly face to face with socialistic
questions. The contrast between the classes and the masses, between rich and poor, is not yet quite so sharp in this vast, fertile,
and developing continent, with less than twenty persons per square
mile, as in crowded little Britain, with fifteen times that number
and no territory unoccupied. Perhaps the "Pall Mall Gazette" in
its issue of September 5 puts most pithily the objections that have
been raised to what the English have been pleased to call "The
Gospel of Wealth." I quote: "Great fortunes, says Mr. Carnegie,
are great blessings to a community, because such and such things

may be done with them. Well, but they are also a great curse, for such and such things are done with them. Mr. Carnegie's preaching, in other words, is altogether vitiated by Mr. Benzon's practice.[8] The gospel of wealth is killed by the acts."

To this the reply seems obvious: the gospel of Christianity is also killed by the acts. The same objection that is urged against the gospel of wealth lies against the commandment, "Thou shalt not steal." It is no argument against a gospel that it is not lived up to; indeed, it is an argument in its favor, for a gospel must be higher than the prevailing standard. It is no argument against a law that it is broken: in that disobedience lies the reason for making and maintaining the law; the law which is never to be broken is never required.

Undoubtedly the most notable incident in regard to "The Gospel of Wealth" is that it was fortunate enough to attract the attention of Mr. Gladstone, and bring forth the following note from him: "I have asked Mr. Lloyd Bryce[9] [*North American Review*] kindly to allow the republication in this country of the extremely interesting article on 'Wealth' by Mr. Andrew Carnegie, which has just appeared in America." This resulted in the publication of the article in several newspapers and periodicals, and an enterprising publisher issued it in pamphlet form, dedicated by permission to Mr. Gladstone.

All this is most encouraging, proving as it does that society is alive to the great issue involved, and is in a receptive mood. Your request, Mr. Editor, that I should continue the subject and point out the best fields for the use of surplus wealth, may be taken as further proof that whether the ideas promulgated are to be received or rejected, they are at least certain to obtain a hearing.

The first article held that there is but one right mode of using enormous fortunes—namely, that the possessors from time to time during their own lives should so administer these as to promote the permanent good of the communities from which they were gathered. It was held that public sentiment would soon say of one who died possessed of available wealth which he was free to administer: "The man who dies thus rich dies disgraced."

The purpose of this paper is to present some of the best methods of performing this duty of adminstering surplus wealth for the good of the people. The first requisite for a really good use of wealth by the millionaire who has accepted the gospel which proclaims him only a trustee of the surplus that comes to him, is to take care that the purposes for which he spends it shall not have a degrading, pauperizing tendency upon its recipients, but that his trust shall be so administered as to stimulate the best and most aspiring poor of the community to further efforts for their own improvement. It is not the irreclaimably destitute, shiftless, and worthless which it is truly beneficial or truly benevolent for the individual to attempt to reach and improve. For these there exists the refuge provided by the city or the State, where they can be sheltered, fed, clothed, and kept in comfortable existence, and—most important of all— where they can be isolated from the well-doing and industrious poor, who are liable to be demoralized by contact with these unfortunates. One man or woman who succeeds in living comfortably by begging is more dangerous to society, and a greater obstacle to the progress of humanity, than a score of wordy Socialists. The individual administrator of surplus wealth has as his charge the industrious and ambitious; not those who need everything done for them, but those who, being most anxious and able to help themselves, deserve and will be benefited by help from others and by the extension of their opportunities by the aid of the philanthropic rich.

It is ever to be remembered that one of the chief obstacles which the philanthropist meets in his efforts to do real and permanent good in this world, is the practice of indiscriminate giving; and the duty of the millionaire is to resolve to cease giving to objects that are not clearly proved to his satisfaction to be deserving. He must remember Mr. Rice's[10] belief, that nine hundred and fifty out of every thousand dollars bestowed to-day upon so-called charity had better be thrown into the sea. As far as my experience of the wealthy extends, it is unnecessary to urge them to give of their super-abundance in charity so called. Greater good for the race is to be achieved by inducing them to cease impulsive and injurious giving. As a rule, the sins of millionaires in this respect are not those of omission, but of commission, because they do not take time to think, and chiefly because it is much easier to give than to refuse. Those who have surplus wealth give millions every year which produce more evil than good, and really retard the progress of the people, because most of the forms in vogue to-day for benefiting mankind only tend to spread among the poor a spirit of dependence upon alms, when what is essential for progress is that they should be inspired to depend upon their own exertions. The miser millionaire who hoards his wealth does less injury to society than the careless millionaire who squanders his unwisely, even if he does so under cover of the mantle of sacred charity. The man who gives to the individual beggar commits a grave offense, but there are many societies and institutions soliciting alms, to aid which is none the less injurious to the community. These are as corrupting as individual beggars. Plutarch's "Morals" contains this lesson: "A beggar asking an alms of a Lacedæmonian, he said: 'Well, should I give thee anything, thou wilt be the greater beggar, for he that first gave thee money made thee idle, and is the cause of this base and dishonorable way of living.'" As I know them, there are few millionaires, very few indeed, who are clear of the sin of having made beggars.

Bearing in mind these considerations, let us endeavor to present some of the best uses to which a millionaire can devote the surplus of which he should regard himself as only the trustee.

First. Standing apart by itself there is the founding of a university by men enormously rich, such men as must necessarily be few in any country. Perhaps the greatest sum ever given by an individual for any purpose is the gift of Senator Stanford, who undertakes to establish a complete university upon the Pacific coast, where he amassed his enormous fortune, which is said to involve the expenditure of ten millions of dollars, and upon which he may be expected to bestow twenty millions of his surplus. He is to be envied. A thousand years hence some orator, speaking his praise upon the then crowded shores of the Pacific, may thus adapt Griffith's eulogy of Wolsey:

> In bestowing, madam,
> He was most princely. Ever witness for him
> This seat of learning, . . .
>   though unfinished, yet so famous.
> So excellent in art, and still so rising,
> That Christendom shall ever speak his virtue.[11]

Here is a noble use of wealth. We have many such institutions,— Johns Hopkins, Cornell, Packer, and others,[12]—but most of these have only been bequeathed, and it is impossible to extol any man greatly for simply leaving what he cannot take with him. Cooper and Pratt and Stanford, and others of this class, deserve credit and admiration as much for the time and attention given during their lives as for their expenditure upon their respective monuments.

We cannot think of the Pacific coast without recalling another important work of a different character which has recently been established there—the Lick Observatory.[13] If any millionaire be interested in the ennobling study of astronomy,—and there should be and would be such if they but gave the subject the slightest attention,—here is an example which could well be followed, for the progress made in astronomical instruments and appliances is so great and continuous that every few years a new telescope might be judiciously given to one of the observatories upon this continent, the last being always the largest and the best, and certain to carry further and further the knowledge of the universe and of our relation to it here upon the earth. As one among many of the good deeds of the late Mr. Thaw of Pittsburg [sic], his constant support of the observatory there may be mentioned. This observatory enabled Professor Langley to make his wonderful discoveries. He is now at the head of the Smithsonian Institution, a worthy successor to Professor Henry. Connected with him was Mr. Braeshier of Pittsburg, whose instruments are in most of the principal observatories of the world. He was a common millwright, but Mr. Thaw recognized his genius and was his main support through trying days. This common workman has been made a professor by one of the foremost scientific bodies of the world. In applying part of his surplus in aiding these two now famous men, the millionaire Thaw did a noble work. Their joint labors have brought great credit, and are destined to bring still greater credit, upon their country in every scientific center throughout the world.[14]

It is reserved for very few to found universities, and, indeed, the use for many, or perhaps, any, new universities does not exist. More good is henceforth to be accomplished by adding to and extending those in existence. But in this department a wide field remains for the millionaire as distinguished from the Croesus among millionaires. The gifts to Yale University have been many, but there is plenty of room for others. The School of Fine Arts, founded by Mr. Street, the Sheffield Scientific School, endowed by Mr. Sheffield, and Professor Loomis's fund for the observatory, are fine examples. Mrs. C. J. Osborne's building for reading and recitation is to be regarded with especial pleasure as being the wise gift of a woman.[15] Harvard University has not been forgotten; the Peabody Museum and the halls of Wells, Matthews, and Thayer may be cited. Sever Hall is worthy of special mention, as showing what a genius like Richardson could do with the small sum of a hundred thousand dollars.[16] The Vanderbilt University, at Nashville, Tennessee, may be mentioned as a true product of the gospel of wealth. It was established by the members of the Vanderbilt family[17] during their lives—mark this vital feature, during their lives; for nothing counts for much that is left by a man at his death. Such funds are torn from him, not given by him. If any millionaire be at a loss to know how to accomplish great and indisputable good with his surplus, here is a field which can never be fully occupied, for the wants of our universities increase with the development of the country.

Second. The result of my own study of the question, What is the best gift which can be given to a community? is that a free library occupies the first place, provided the community will accept and maintain it as a public institution, as much a part of the city property as its public schools, and, indeed, an adjunct to these. It is, no doubt, possible that my own personal experience may have led me to value a free library beyond all other forms of beneficence. When I was a working-boy in Pittsburg, Colonel Anderson of Allegheny—a name I can never speak without feelings of devotional gratitude—opened his little library of four hundred books to boys. Every Saturday afternoon he was in attendance at his house to exchange books. No one but he who has felt it can ever know the intense longing with which the arrival of Saturday was awaited, that a new book might be had. My brother and Mr. Phipps,[18] who have been my principal business partners through life, shared with me Colonel Anderson's precious generosity, and it was when reveling in the treasures which he opened to us that I resolved, if ever wealth came to me, that it should be used to establish free libraries, that other poor boys might receive opportunities similar to those for which we were indebted to that noble man.

Great Britain has been foremost in appreciating the value of free libraries for its people. Parliament passed an act permitting towns and cities to establish and maintain these as municipal institutions;

whenever the people of any town or city voted to accept the provisions of the act, the authorities were authorized to tax the community to the extent of one penny in the pound valuation. Most
of the towns already have free libraries under this act. Many of
these are the gifts of rich men, whose funds have been used for
the building, and in some cases for the books also, the communities
being required to maintain and to develop the libraries. And to
this feature I attribute most of their usefulness. An endowed institution is liable to become the prey of a clique. The public ceases
to take interest in it, or rather, never acquires interest in it. The
rule has been violated which requires the recipients to help themselves. Everything has been done for the community instead of its
being only helped to help itself, and good results rarely ensue.

Many free libraries have been established in our country, but
none that I know of with such wisdom as the Pratt Library in
Baltimore. Mr. Pratt built and presented the library to the city of
Baltimore, with the balance of cash handed over; the total cost
was one million dollars, upon which he required the city to pay
five per cent, per annum, fifty thousand dollars per year, to trustees
for the maintenance and development of the library and its branch-
es. During 1888 430,217 books were distributed; 37,196 people
of Baltimore are registered upon the books as readers. And it is
safe to say that 37,000 frequenters of the Pratt Library are of more
value to Baltimore, to the State, and to the country, than all the
inert, lazy, and hopelessly poor in the whole nation. And it may
further be safely said that, by placing books within the reach of
37,000 aspiring people which they were anxious to obtain, Mr.
Pratt has done more for the genuine progress of the people than
has been done by all the contributions of all the millionaires and
rich people to help those who cannot or will not help themselves.
The one wise administrator of his surplus has poured a fertilizing
stream upon soil that was ready to receive it and return a hun-
dredfold. The many squanderers have not only poured their streams
into sieves which can never be filled—they have done worse; they
have poured them into stagnant sewers that breed the diseases which
most afflict the body politic. And this is not all. The million dollars
of which Mr. Pratt has made so grand a use are something, but
there is something greater still. When the fifth branch library was
opened in Baltimore, the speaker said:

Whatever may have been done in these four years, it is my pleasure to acknowledge that much, very much, is due to the earnest interest, the wise counsels, and the practical suggestions of Mr. Pratt. He never seemed to feel that the mere donation of great wealth for the benefit of his fellow-citizens was all that would be asked of him, but he wisely labored to make its application as comprehensive and effective as possible. Thus he constantly lightened burdens that were, at times, very heavy, brought good cheer and bright sunshine when clouds flitted across the sky, and made every officer and employee feel that good work was appreciated, and loyal devotion to duty would receive hearty commendation.

This is the finest picture I have ever seen of any of the millionaire class. As here depicted, Mr. Pratt is the ideal disciple of the gospel of wealth. We need have no fear that the mass of toilers will fail to recognize in such as he their best leaders and their most invaluable allies; for the problem of poverty and wealth, of employer and employed, will be practically solved whenever the time of the few is given, and their wealth is administered during their lives, for the best good of that portion of the community which has not been burdened with the responsibilities which attend the possession of wealth. We shall have no antagonism between classes when that day comes, for the high and the low, the rich and the poor, shall then indeed be brothers.

No millionaire will go far wrong in his search for one of the best forms for the use of his surplus who chooses to establish a free library in any community that is willing to maintain and develop it. John Bright's[19] words should ring in his ear: "It is impossible for any man to bestow a greater benefit upon a young man than to give him access to books in a free library." Closely allied to the library, and, where possible, attached to it, there should be rooms for an art-gallery and museum, and a hall for such lectures and instruction as are provided in the Cooper Union. The traveler upon the Continent is surprised to find that every town of importance has its art-gallery and museum; these may be large or small, but each has a receptacle for the treasures of the locality, in which are constantly being placed valuable gifts and bequests. The Free Library and Art Gallery of Birmingham are remarkable among such institutions, and every now and then a rich man adds to their value by presenting books, fine pictures, or other works of art. All that our cities require, to begin with, is a proper fire-proof building. Their citizens who travel will send to it rare and costly things from every quarter of the globe they visit, while those who remain at home will give or bequeath to it of their treasures. In this way collections will grow until our cities will ultimately be able to boast of permanent exhibitions from which their own citizens will derive incalculable benefit, and which they will be proud to show to visitors. In the Metropolitan Museum of Art in New York we have made an excellent beginning. Here is another avenue for the proper use of surplus wealth.

Third. We have another most important department in which great sums can be worthily used—the founding or extension of hospitals, medical colleges, laboratories, and other institutions connected with the alleviation of human suffering, and especially with the prevention rather than with the cure of human ills. There is no danger of pauperizing a community in giving for such purposes, because such institutions relieve temporary ailments or shelter only those who are hopeless invalids. What better gift than a hospital can be given to a community that is without one?—the gift being conditioned upon its proper maintenance by the community in its corporate capacity. If hospital accommodation already exists, no better method for using surplus wealth can be found than in making additions to it. The late Mr. Vanderbilt's gift of half a million dollars to the Medical Department of Columbia College for a chemical laboratory was one of the wisest possible uses of wealth.[20] It strikes at the prevention of disease by penetrating into its causes. Several others have established such laboratories, but the need for them is still great.

If there be a millionaire in the land who is at a loss what to do with the surplus that has been committed to him as trustee, let him investigate the good that is flowing from these chemical laboratories. No medical college is complete without its laboratory. As with universities, so with medical colleges: it is not new institutions that are required, but additional means for the more thorough equipment of those that exist. The forms that benefactions to these may wisely take are numerous, but probably none is more useful than that adopted by Mr. Osborne when he built a school for training female nurses at Bellevue College.[21] If from all gifts there flows one half of the good that comes from this wise use of a millionaire's surplus, the most exacting may well be satisfied. Only those who have passed through a lingering and dangerous illness can rate at their true value the care, skill, and attendance of trained female nurses. Their employment as nurses has enlarged the sphere and influence of woman. It is not to be wondered at that a senator of the United States, and a physician distinguished in this country for having received the highest distinctions abroad, should recently have found their wives in this class.

Fourth. In the very front rank of benefactions public parks should be placed, always provided that the community undertakes to maintain, beautify, and preserve them inviolate. No more useful or more beautiful monument can be left by any man than a park for the city in which he was born or in which he has long lived, nor can the community pay a more graceful tribute to the citizen who presents it than to give his name to the gift. Mrs. Schenley's gift last month of a large park to the city of Pittsburg deserves to be noted. This lady, although born in Pittsburg, married an English gentleman while yet in her teens. It is forty years and more since she took up her residence in London among the titled and the wealthy of the world's metropolis, but still she turns to the home of her childhood and by means of Schenley Park links her name with it forever.[22] A noble use this of great wealth by one who thus becomes her own administrator. If a park be already provided, there is still room for many judicious gifts in connection with it. Mr. Phipps of Allegheny has given conservatories to the park there, which are visited by many every day of the week, and crowded by thousands of working-people every Sunday; for, with rare wisdom, he has stipulated as a condition of the gift that the conservatories shall be open on Sundays. The result of his experiment has been so gratifying that he finds himself justified in adding to them from his surplus, as he is doing largely this year. To lovers of flowers among the wealthy I commend a study of what is possible for them to do in the line of Mr. Phipps's example; and may they please note that Mr. Phipps is a wise as well as a liberal giver, for he requires the city to maintain these conservatories, and thus secures for them forever the public ownership, the public interest, and the public criticism of their management. Had he undertaken to manage and maintain them, it is probable that popular interest in the gift would never have been awakened.

The parks and pleasure-grounds of small towns throughout Europe are not less surprising than their libraries, museums, and art-galleries. I saw nothing more pleasing during my recent travels than the hill at Bergen, in Norway. It has been converted into one of the most picturesque of pleasuregrounds; fountains, cascades, waterfalls, delightful arbors, fine terraces, and statues adorn what was before a barren mountain-side. Here is a field worthy of study by the millionaire who would confer a lasting benefit upon his fellows. Another beautiful instance of the right use of wealth in the direction of making cities more and more attractive is to be found in Dresden. The owner of the leading paper there bequeathed its revenues forever to the city, to be used in beautifying it. An art committee decides, from time to time, what new artistic feature is to be introduced, or what hideous feature is to be changed, and as the revenues accrue, they are expended in this direction. Thus, through the gift of this patriotic newspaper proprietor his native city of Dresden is fast becoming one of the most artistic places of residence in the whole world. A work having been completed, it devolves upon the city to maintain it forever. May I be excused if I commend to our millionaire newspaper proprietors the example of their colleague in the capital of Saxony?

Scarcely a city of any magnitude in the older countries is without many structures and features of great beauty. Much has been spent upon ornament, decoration, and architectural effect. We are still far behind in these things upon this side of the Atlantic. Our Republic is great in some things—in material development unrivaled; but let us always remember that in art and in the finer touches we have scarcely yet taken a place. Had the exquisite Memorial Arch recently erected temporarily in New York been shown in Dresden, the art committee there would probably have been enabled, from the revenue of the newspaper given by its owner for just such purposes, to order its permanent erection to adorn the city forever.*

While the bestowal of a park upon a community will be universally approved as one of the best uses for surplus wealth, in embracing such additions to it as conservatories, or in advocating

*Popular subscriptions have accomplished this result in the case referred to (the Washington Monument), and two other memorial arches have been designed and are to be erected here.—ED. [Note in original edition.]

the building of memorial arches and works of adornment, it is probable that many will think I go too far, and consider these somewhat fanciful. The material good to flow from them may not be so directly visible; but let not any practical mind, intent only upon material good, depreciate the value of wealth given for these or for kindred esthetic purposes as being useless as far as the mass of the people and their needs are concerned. As with libraries and museums, so with these more distinctively artistic works: they perform their great use when they reach the best of the masses of the people. It is better to reach and touch the sentiment for beauty in the naturally bright minds of this class than to pander to those incapable of being so touched. For what the improver of the race must endeavor is to reach those who have the divine spark ever so feebly developed, that it may be strengthened and grow. For my part, I think Mr. Phipps put his money to better use in giving the working-men of Allegheny conservatories filled with beautiful flowers, orchids, and aquatic plants, which they, with their wives and children, can enjoy in their spare hours, and upon which they can feed their love for the beautiful, than if he had given his surplus money to furnish them with bread; for those in health who cannot earn their bread are scarcely worth considering by the individual giver, the care of such being the duty of the State. The man who erects in a city a conservatory or a truly artistic arch, statue, or fountain, makes a wise use of his surplus. "Man does not live by bread alone."

Fifth. We have another good use for surplus wealth in providing our cities with halls suitable for meetings of all kinds, and for concerts of elevating music. Our cities are rarely possessed of halls for these purposes, being in this respect also very far behind European cities. Springer Hall, in Cincinnati, a valuable addition to the city, was largely the gift of Mr. Springer, who was not content to bequeath funds from his estate at death, but gave during his life, and, in addition, gave—what was equally important—his time and business ability to insure the successful results which have been achieved.[23] The gift of a hall to any city lacking one is an excellent use for surplus wealth for the good of a community. The reason why the people have only one instructive and elevating, or even amusing, entertainment when a dozen would be highly beneficial, is that the rent of a hall, even when suitable hall exists, which is rare, is so great as to prevent managers from running the risk of financial failure. If every city in our land owned a hall which could be given or rented for a small sum for such gatherings as a committee or the mayor of the city judged advantageous, the people could be furnished with proper lectures, amusements, and concerts at an exceedingly small cost. The town halls of European cities, many of which have organs, are of inestimable value to the people, utilized as they are in the manner suggested. Let no one underrate the influence of entertainments of an elevating or even of an amusing character, for these do much to make the lives of the people happier and their natures better. If any millionaire born in a small village which has now become a great city is prompted in the day of his success to do something for his birthplace with part of his surplus, his grateful remembrance cannot take a form more useful than that of a public hall with an organ, provided the city agrees to maintain and use it.

Sixth. In another respect we are still much behind Europe. A form of benevolence which is not uncommon there is providing swimming-baths for the people. The donors of these have been wise enough to require the city benefited to maintain them at its own expense, and as proof of the contention that everything should never be done for any one or for any community, but that the recipients should invariably be called upon to do a part, it is significant that it is found essential for the popular success of these healthful establishments to exact a nominal charge for their use. In many cities, however, the school-children are admitted free at fixed hours upon certain days; different hours being fixed for the boys and the girls to use the great swimming-baths, hours or days being also fixed for the use of these baths by women. In addition to the highly beneficial effect of these institutions upon the public health in inland cities, the young of both sexes are thus taught to swim. Swimming clubs are organized, and matches are frequent, at which medals and prizes are given. The reports published by the various swimming-bath establishments throughout Great Britain are filled with instances of lives saved because those who fortunately escaped shipwreck had been taught to swim in the baths; and not a few instances are given in which the pupils of certain bathing establishments have saved the lives of others. If any disciple of the gospel of wealth gives his favorite city large swimming and private baths, provided the municipality undertakes their management as a city affair, he will never be called to account for an improper use of the funds intrusted to him.

Seventh. Churches as fields for the use of surplus wealth have purposely been reserved for the last, because, these being sectarian, every man will be governed in his action in regard to them by his own attachments; therefore gifts to churches, it may be said, are not, in one sense, gifts to the community at large, but to special classes. Nevertheless, every millionaire may know of a district where the little cheap, uncomfortable, and altogether unworthy wooden structure stands at the cross-roads, in which the whole neighborhood gathers on Sunday, and which, independently of the form of the doctrines taught, is the center of social life and source of neighborly feeling. The administrator of wealth makes a good use of a part of his surplus if he replaces that building with a permanent structure of brick, stone, or granite, up whose sides the honeysuckle and columbine may climb, and from whose tower the sweet-tolling bell may sound. The millionaire should not figure how cheaply this structure can be built, but how perfect it can be made. If he has the money, it should be made a gem, for the educating influence of a pure and noble specimen of architecture, built, as the pyramids were built, to stand for ages, is not to be measured by dollars. Every farmer's home, heart, and mind in the district will be influenced by the beauty and grandeur of the church; and many a bright boy, gazing enraptured upon its richly colored windows and entranced by the celestial voice of the organ, will there receive his first message from and in spirit be carried away to the beautiful and enchanting realm which lies far from the material and prosaic conditions which surround him in this workaday world—a real world, this new realm, vague and undefined though its boundaries be. Once within its magic circle, its denizens live there an inner life more precious than the external, and all their days and all their ways; their triumphs and their trials, and all they see, and all they hear, and all they think, and all they do, are hallowed by the radiance which shines from afar upon this inner life, glorifying everything, and keeping all right within. But having given the building, the donor should stop there; the support of the church should be upon its own people. There is not much genuine religion in the congregation or much good to come from the church which is not supported at home.

Many other avenues for the wise expenditure of surplus wealth might be indicated. I enumerate but a few—a very few—of the many fields which are open, and only those in which great or considerable sums can be judiciously used. It is not the privilege, however, of millionaires alone to work for or aid measures which are certain to benefit the community. Every one who has but a small surplus above his moderate wants may share this privilege with his richer brothers, and those without surplus can give at least a part of their time, which is usually as important as funds, and often more so.

It is not expected, neither is it desirable, that there should be general concurrence as to the best possible use of surplus wealth. For different men and different localities there are different uses. What commends itself most highly to the judgment of the administrator is the best use for him, for his heart should be in the work. It is as important in administering wealth as it is in any other branch of a man's work that he should be enthusiastically devoted to it and feel that in the field selected his work lies.

Besides this, there is room and need for all kinds of wise benefactions for the common weal. The man who builds a university, library, or laboratory performs no more useful work than he who elects to devote himself and his surplus means to the adornment of a park, the gathering together of a collection of pictures for the public, or the building of a memorial arch. These are all true laborers in the vineyard. The only point required by the gospel of wealth is that the surplus which accrues from time to time in the hands of a man should be administered by him in his own lifetime for that purpose which is seen by him, as trustee, to be best for the good of the people. To leave at death what he cannot take away, and place upon others the burden of the work which it was his own duty to perform, is to do nothing worthy. This requires no sacrifice, nor any sense of duty to his fellows.

Time was when the words concerning the rich man entering the kingdom of heaven were regarded as a hard saying. To-day, when all questions are probed to the bottom and the standards of faith receive the most liberal interpretations, the startling verse has been relegated to the rear, to await the next kindly revision as one of those things which cannot be quite understood, but which, meanwhile, it is carefully to be noted, are not to be understood literally. But is it so very improbable that the next stage of thought is to restore the doctrine in all its pristine purity and force, as being in perfect harmony with sound ideas upon the subject of wealth and poverty, the rich and the poor, and the contrasts everywhere seen and deplored? In Christ's day, it is evident, reformers were against the wealthy. It is none the less evident that we are fast recurring to that position to-day; and there will be nothing to surprise the student of sociological development if society should soon approve the text which has caused so much anxiety: "It is easier for a camel to enter the eye of a needle than for a rich man to enter the kingdom of heaven." Even if the needle were the small casement at the gates, the words betoken serious difficulty for the rich. It will be but a step for the theologian from the doctrine that he who dies rich dies disgraced, to that which brings upon the man punishment or deprivation hereafter.

The gospel of wealth but echoes Christ's words. It calls upon the millionaire to sell all that he hath and give it in the highest and best form to the poor by administering his estate himself for the good of his fellows, before he is called upon to lie down and rest upon the bosom of Mother Earth. So doing, he will approach his end no longer the ignoble hoarder of useless millions; poor, very poor indeed, in money, but rich, very rich, twenty times a millionaire still, in the affection, gratitude, and admiration of his fellow-men, and—sweeter far—soothed and sustained by the still, small voice within, which, whispering, tells him that, because he has lived, perhaps one small part of the great world has been bettered just a little. This much is sure: against such riches as these no bar will be found at the gates of Paradise.

Notes

1. Published originally in the *North American Review,* CXLVIII (June 1889), 653–664, and CXLIX (December 1889), 682–698. Carnegie did not devise the appropriate and fetching title this essay now bears. He called it "Wealth." William T. Stead, editor of the *Pall Mall Gazette,* supplied the heading "The Gospel of Wealth." The personally dramatic circum-

stances under which the editor of the *North American Review* accepted the original article highly appealed to Carnegie's vanity and bent for personal excitement. He reported the circumstances in the first two paragraphs of his second periodical article, "The Best Fields for Philanthropy," which appeared in the *Review* in December 1889. As the latter article is here reprinted, Carnegie omitted this episode and began with the third paragraph of the original. There were also other minor changes from the original essay.

2. Carnegie is referring to Emanuel Swedenborg's (1688–1772) mystic theology expressed in his work *Heaven and Hell*.

3. Inheritance taxes have historically taken many forms. They may be progressively heavier depending on the size of the transferred estate; they may vary with the relationship of the beneficiary to the testator; they may be levied upon different kinds of property. By the late eighties England had carried the system of "death duties," purportedly a Gladstonian designation, farther than any other nation. By 1890 only six American states levied taxes of one sort or another on inheritances; and federal resort to inheritance taxation had been generally a temporary feature of emergency war financing. By 1900 twenty-one states had inheritance taxes.

4. Portia's judgment in *Merchant of Venice*, Act IV, scene 1.

5. Cooper Union, which celebrated in 1959 the centenary of its opening, was the chief philanthropic undertaking of Peter Cooper (1791–1883). A resident of New York, whose main iron mills were in New Jersey, Cooper was moved to establish an institution providing for those of little means an education in pure and applied science. The Union, though its activities soon embraced a wide variety of intellectual interests, stressed contributions "to the useful purposes of life" and adult education. The Union's building at 3rd Avenue and 7th Street appropriately embodied many structural innovations. Before his death Cooper had given the Union upwards of $900,000. In 1902 Carnegie gave $600,000 to its endowment.

6. Samuel J. Tilden (1814–1886), New Yorker, able corporation lawyer, loser of the disputed presidential election of 1876, bequeathed a considerable share of his large estate "to establish and maintain a free public library and reading room in the City of New York." To accomplish this end his executors were to incorporate a Tilden Trust. Family heirs contested the will, and in a series of decisions—possibly animated by political considerations—various New York courts upset the testator's instructions. Though the Tilden Trust was incorporated in 1887 and the executors settled with the heirs in 1892, the estate was formally in the hands of executors until 1930. With about $2,250,000 in hand for a library, the Tilden Trust amalgamated in 1901 with the Astor and Lenox Libraries to form the New York Public Library. The present classical building on Fifth Avenue, housing the library, was the fruit of this settlement.

7. Of this cluster of philanthropists, Enoch Pratt (1808–1896) was a New Englander who moved to Baltimore and accumulated a fortune as a merchant of iron products and as a general investor. In the eighties he

constructed a library building and gave it along with an endowment of over $800,000 to the City of Baltimore. Carnegie once hailed Pratt as "my pioneer." Charles Pratt (1830–1891), also a New Englander, moved to New York and established a firm to deal in paints and oils. Sensing in the sixties the importance of petroleum, he was one of the founders of Charles Pratt and Company; the concern refined oil on Long Island. When the Rockefeller interests acquired this business in 1874, Pratt became a member of the high command in Standard Oil. In 1887 his funds and educational acumen led to the opening of the Pratt Institute in Brooklyn, a secondary school for training in the trades. He also established the Pratt Institute Free Library, "the first free public library in either Brooklyn or New York." Leland Stanford (1824–1893), a New Yorker, moved to California, prospered as a wholesale merchant in Sacramento, was Civil War Governor of the State, and one of the "Big Four" associated in promoting, organizing, financing, and building the Central Pacific, the western link of the first transcontinental railroad. Subsequently he became a pioneer in the Southern Pacific Railroad and a United State Senator. In 1884, the death of an only son at the age of fifteen shattered Stanford and his wife. After personal reflection and after seeking advice among educators, the parents founded Leland Stanford Junior University on their Palo Alto "farm." The new institution charged no tuition and emphasized preparation for the practical affairs of life. For many years the Stanfords concerned themselves with the details of university administration, whether in the architecture of the buildings or the character of appointments.

8. Ernest Benzon, commonly known as the "Jubilee plunger," was an English rogue of the fin-de-siècle variety. His career apparently came to grief on the Riviera when he was brought into court for forgery or obtaining money under false pretenses.

9. Lloyd Stephens Bryce (1851–1917) was owner and editor of the *North American Review* beginning in 1889. He combined the diverse talents of man of wealth, bon vivant, merchant, and member of Congress.

10. Charles Allen Thorndike Rice (1851–1889), publisher of the *North American Review*, 1886–1889.

11. Quoted inaccurately from *Henry VIII*, Act IV, scene 2, lines 51 ff.

12. In the founding of universities by private wealth in the post-Civil War era, the names of institutions perpetuate the donations and other assistance of Johns Hopkins (1795–1873), a Baltimore philanthropist, and Ezra Cornell (1807–1874), an upstate New Yorker who built a fortune from the telegraph. Asa Packer (1805–1879), a New England youth who emigrated to Pennsylvania, acquired his fortune from transporting and mining coal in the anthracite region. He was a judge and a politician. After the Civil War Packer donated money and land to a new institution, Lehigh University. He originally had in mind a technical institution, but when the school was opened in 1885 its scheme was more traditional. The total of Packer's donations in his lifetime gifts and bequests was over $3,800,000.

13. James Lick (1796–1876), an eccentric who made a fortune from investments in San Francisco real estate and California land, was with difficulty guided by careful advisers to give $700,000 for a telescope "superior to and more powerful than any telescope ever made." Previous to this decision he had never seen a telescope or looked through one and had not even an amateur's acquaintance with astronomy. Eventually the managers of the gift located the Lick observatory on Mt. Hamilton, a wilderness peak in Santa Clara County, and contracted for a 36-inch lens, the largest feasible under the technology of the eighties. The regents of the University of California became the trustees of the Lick observatory.

14. Pittsburgh immediately after the Civil War became a center of astronomical activity and scholarship. A popular subscription had raised funds to build in 1860 the old Allegheny observatory, and five years later it was transferred to the Western University of Pennsylvania (since 1908 the University of Pittsburgh). In 1867 Samuel P. Langley (1834–1906), a man of immense erudition and scientific originality, became director of the observatory and professor of physics and astronomy. Twenty years later Langley became the third secretary of the Smithsonian Institution. Meanwhile, John Alfred Brashear (1840–1920)—one of many variant spellings— a Pittsburgh machinist who in his youth had been inspired by his maternal grandfather with a love of the stars, had built his own telescope and had attracted the attention of Langley. William Thaw, who had acquired wealth as a freight forwarder and Pennsylvania Railroad official and investor, was a director of Western University. He financed Langley's researches—the observatory incidentally provided correct time for the railroad—and enabled Brashear to set up in business as a maker of precision instruments and telescopes. Carnegie later selected him as one of three men to draw up plans for the Carnegie Institute of Technology founded in 1905.

15. A series of gifts enlarged the physical facilities and instructional offerings of Yale College. Just before the Civil War Joseph E. Sheffield (1793–1882), a Connecticut man who had made a fortune as a railroad contractor in the West and, out of personal and civic pride, spent some of it financing a needless New England railroad, gave the first of his donations to the Yale Scientific School, renamed the Sheffield Scientific School in 1861. After the War, Augustus R. Street (1791–1866), a New Haven-born Yale graduate, and his wife, a woman of wealth, financed a building for the Yale School of Fine Arts and endowed instruction in a number of areas at Yale. In the late eighties Elias Loomis (1811–1889), who had made a fortune as author of books in the field of natural science, bequeathed $300,000 to Yale. Mrs. Miriam A. (C. J.) Osborn gave in the eighties a sum for a building for history. Its construction "resulted in the removal of the Fence."

16. Mr. Carnegie's stroll through Harvard produced some inaccurate observations. George Peabody (1795–1869), an American banker in London, donated in 1866, at the suggestion of a Yale nephew, $150,000 for a "Museum and Professorship of American Archaeology and Ethnology." But there is not and never was a Wells Hall. This is a mistake for

Weld Hall, given in 1872 by W. F. Weld, a Boston financier, in memory of his brother. Like Weld, the other "halls" were dormitories. Matthews Hall was the gift in 1872 of Nathan Matthews (1854–1927), a Boston merchant; Thayer Hall, of Nathanial Thayer (1808–1883), a member of a Boston investment banking house, in memory of his brother. Colonel James W. Sever, a shoeman in southeastern Massachusetts, bequeathed $100,000 for a hall to be named for the family. Sever Hall is a classroom building.

17. The first Vanderbilt gift to the Central University of the Methodist Episcopal Church of the South at Nashville came from Cornelius ("The Commodore") Vanderbilt (1794–1877), veteran steamship tycoon and virtually a synonym for the New York Central Railroad. Since the Commodore became Vanderbilt's benefactor in a decidedly offhand manner, Carnegie's note of admiration is surprising. In time the Commodore's descendants generously supplemented his original benefaction.

18. Thomas M. Carnegie (1843–1886), a younger brother of Andrew, followed a somewhat similar career. Henry Phipps, Jr. (1839–1930), was a boyhood neighbor and chum of Andrew. Tom Carnegie and Phipps early entered the iron business. Tom died in 1886; Phipps stayed with the Carnegie firm until its acquisition by United States Steel in 1901. His money supported a wide variety of philanthropic undertakings from public baths to psychiatric institutes.

19. The noted British liberal statesman, reformer, and orator (1811–1889), who believed strongly in self-education.

20. Gifts from the Vanderbilts enabled Columbia's College of Physicians and Surgeons in the eighties to move to a new location and plant on West 59th Street. W. H. Vanderbilt (1821–1885), the son of the Commodore and an exceedingly able business man in his own right, was for the moment the chief of the Vanderbilt givers.

21. William Henry Osborn (1820–1894), reorganizer and financial savior of the Illinois Central Railroad, after his retirement in 1882 became interested in aiding medical institutions, among which was the Bellevue Training School for Nurses in New York City.

22. Pittsburgh advocates of parks induced Mrs. Mary E. Schenley to donate 300 acres for a park and the city purchased for $200,000 an additional acreage. In addition to facilities for sports and beauty, Schenley Park was the site of the Phipps conservatories, the first Carnegie Pittsburgh Library, and the Carnegie Institute.

23. Reuben R. Springer (1800–1884), a successful investor in real estate and railroads, gave the major share of the money for the erection of the Cincinnati Music Hall. Opened in 1878, this red brick, semi-Gothic building housed the Cincinnati Music Festival and later the Cincinnati Symphony Orchestra. Perhaps inspired by this example, Andrew Carnegie in 1892 built the New York Music Hall on 57th Street. Since the latter name repelled European artists, who associated it with vaudeville, it was changed to Carnegie Hall.

Andrew Carnegie and His Gospel of Philanthropy

A STUDY IN THE ETHICS OF RESPONSIBILITY

BARRY D. KARL

Andrew Carnegie was part of a generation of men whose enormous wealth seemed to come to them as something of a surprise. While they never acknowledged that fact as such, their periodic efforts to explain the logic and inevitability of their wealth to others might suggest it. Their memoirs emphasize their humble beginnings, in some senses too much so. And even a close look at their analysis of the incremental steps that led to the accumulation of what were, after all, remarkable financial resources by any historical standard we want to apply, leaves us with holes they have to help us fill with what sometimes seem fictions. Their stories are designed to impress us, and quite rightly, with the fact that in an age filled with criticism of the way wealth had come to the wealthy, they were honest men, simple in their beliefs, and responsible to the less well off in the world around them.

It might be useful to reconstruct, insofar as a historian can, that very complex world of transformation that sometimes seems clearer to us than it did to them. For what may seem obvious to later observers is their gift to us, the perpetuation of their philanthropic lives, and that may obscure the struggle they spent those lives trying to understand. They gambled with technological resources their youth gave them the courage to exploit and natural resources their contemporaries understood no better than they did.

Some of the basic historical outlines can be drawn without reference to their various rationalizations. Their wealth was a product

Some of the basic historical outlines can be drawn without reference to their various rationalizations. Their wealth was a product of the rapid post–Civil War expansion of the United States. That era of unprecedented growth includes a revolution in transcontinental transportation and communication, the exploration and discovery of new natural resources and the invention of new uses for them, and the organization of western territories into states. The wealth of the men who were able to benefit from so remarkable a transformation of resources was thus a historical phenomenon that may seem oddly independent of them as individuals. The rewards were there to reap. The nation would have had its steel and oil industries with or without the men whose names we now associate with them.

This is not to suggest any historical inevitability that would denigrate their remarkable contributions. It is to argue that their organization of what they did and their utilization of their particular kind of business judgment and moral perspicacity may be what we need most to understand. For it is certainly there that the names of Carnegie and Rockefeller have a special place in the history of their generation. Whether or not they intended to, and at times in spite of their intentions, they helped create the system of national industrial and economic management we live with today. Many of the elements that make it unique among such systems are attributable to them.

Carnegie was considerably more articulate in formulating his explanations than his modest education seemed to justify. Even John D. Rockefeller's late memoir is less aggressively revealing and more limited in its theorizing about the causes of their success. The fact that we may be more grateful to Carnegie for such moments of self-rationalization than he would have been to us were our circumstances reversed may be one of the essential and still inexplicable elements in describing the feelings of nineteenth century leaders in late nineteenth American economic history. Most Americans looked upon them with a mixture of criticism and admiration neither man ever understood, particularly as each of them surveyed their gifts to American society; but they absorbed the criticism as best they could, accepted the admiration with a certain amount of cautious gratitude, and continued giving their gifts.

We tend not to remember the methods they were forced to create in a financial world that offered them more in the way of pitfalls than supportive routes. They worked without most of the financial networks we take for granted and none of the safety nets.[1] They mistrusted the big American subsidiaries of international banks, indeed, any bank so distant they could not call its owners friends,[2] and the stock market, which was only then coming into being as the major center of financial transaction it is today. They sought funds for long term investment and looked with something close to horror on the idea of buying and selling stocks that did not reflect the value of their management.[3] They placed great emphasis on the hiring of trustworthy and congenial men; but kept in as much touch with their activities as they thought possible. Most important, perhaps, the financial worlds they built were themselves so extraordinary that they initiated changes in American economic practice that made even those business institutions that might appear to be their successors, new organisms, as Carnegie's Darwinism might have had it, adapt, because of them, to new environments. They themselves stood alone and still do.

Until recently, it has been more or less customary for historians to discount Carnegie's Darwinism as the musing of an old man attracted to an idea he little understood beyond its obvious convenience. Joseph Wall's biography makes Carnegie's philosophy more of a lifetime development that began with a family commitment to Chartism, a British working-class movement of the 1830s and 1840s that sought to democratize Parliament, and moved through his rejection of his father's Swedenborgianism, a religion that emphasized, among many other things, a commitment to nature and science as central factors in the order of things. Both provided a complex philosophical and political set of underpinnings for the Scottish migrant who retained a sense of moral order and militant democracy ("My childhood's desire was, to get to be a man and kill a king," he told William Stead in 1897) that came from a number of levels above the streets.[4] The mother with whom he shared a large part of his adult life assured that.

John D. Rockefeller and his associates, early in their interest in the investigations of oil resources in the west, went to one of the great figures in Pennsylvania oil and asked his advice. He offered to drink every quart of oil that could be found west of the Mississippi River.[5] One laughs at the reponse, but it shows the problems after the Civil War. And it shows the limitations of the expert advice they were forced to depend upon. Most of Rockefeller's associates were Ohio grain merchants, certain of little beyond their training as good bookkeepers and their complex relation to the expanding system of railroads, the merchant bankers who demonstrated their trust in them by providing them with the essential financial resources with which to begin, and their faith in one another as honest men eager to learn and willing to teach one another.

Carnegie's associates were Pittsburgh friends like Henry Clay Frick, a builder of coke ovens and a traveling companion of Andrew Mellon, whose father, Thomas, lent him his first financial stake. Their early European travels together introduced them to the artworks they began purchasing, the first items in the collections these self-taught men were ultimately to turn over to the public in their various forms.[6]

Carnegie's steel empire was the product of a series of innovations in the production of iron, the discovery of the enormous iron deposits in the Lake Superior region in 1844, but for his purposes the introduction of the Bessemer process for the conversion of iron into steel in 1864 was key. The coincidence of that with the demand for rails for the expanding railroad system was what brought the simple telegrapher, in his own eyes at least, to the nineteenth century's great combination in the sources of wealth. He seemed always at the right place at the right time.

Yet the writings of both Carnegie and Rockefeller show them to be acutely aware of the skills required of them, skills in the management of others and in the control of choices in a rapidly expanding world others may have perceived as a chaos. In the later phases of their lives as they rethought what they had done, they placed great emphasis on knowledge, technical training, and the ability of people to trust one another and to accept with caution and a very limited sense of personal appropriateness the justice of the rewards that came to them. Unlike the lonely behemoths represented in films like Orson Welles's *Citizen Kane,* sitting at the end of long tables in monumental castle rooms, having rejected families for the solace of some young beauty, they were far more protective of a family life they were determined to convert to their own concept of their wealth. There were obviously those who did what Welles's hero did, but no Carnegies and few of the Rockefellers were among them.

By the end of the nineteenth century some of them were very well aware of how precarious the whole operation of developing wealth had been. Cornelius Vanderbilt, a steamboat entrepreneur, discovered slightly ahead of contemporaries who still were investing in canals that domestic ships and ferries would not simply connect short rail lines with one another but be replaced by them. He sought help from spiritualists to commune with the souls of railroad and currency manipulators like Jay Gould and Jim Fiske in order to divine the next step. We don't know what advice he got from them, but his rapid buying up of all the rail lines available to him would have made them proud. Again, technological innovation had intervened. The old iron-clad wooden rails that carried the early locomotives were indeed useful only for short distances. Steel wheels running on steel rails dramatically reduced the effects of friction, vastly increasing the distance that could be traveled, the weight that could be carried, and the speed.

Rockefeller and Carnegie by contrast turned to science and education. Margaret Olivia Sage, their chief companion in early modern foundation philanthropy, rejected both mysticism and science and looked to hands-on research in the practical problems of human well-being. The latter three served as models for their colleagues, as well as for a whole generation of new philanthropists whose different consciousnesses of their responsibilities preceded the tax laws that gave modern shape to the institutions they created. The modern foundation was an investment in innovation.

Thus, all were recognizing a common element in acknowledging that what had put them where they were would not continue to work unaided for future generations. Vanderbilt's method may have been self-interested and crude, but it was a statement that still left place for a very real fear of the ambiguous conditions that seemed to touch them all. Panics were like giant earthquakes and the depressions that followed like epidemics that threatened to spread frightening ailments that would invade even their safe environments. Poverty and ignorance endangered stability and advance.

The Vanderbilts gave the grant that expanded the school at Nashville that bears their name, but they maintained the greatest part of their wealth for themselves and their family. Cornelius's son, William's, famous statement, "the public be damned" was the voicing of an inheritance. The castles they built for themselves in Newport, Rhode Island, and Asheville, North Carolina, stand today as monuments to a sense of protected isolation that would later allow their estates to be turned into public places, like the homes of the Japanese emperors, to be visited and admired by ordinary people. The banking community that it took to salvage William's misspoken statement did its work well. Their wealth was for future generations that would face worlds different from the ones they had known and their use of it quite possibly less generous and certainly less opulent in releasing energy for the future.

Andrew Carnegie's original title, "Wealth," was given its final and distinctive polish by his friend, the editor of the *Pall Mall Gazette,* Mr. William T. Stead, and accepted by the editor of the *North American Review* where the essay also appeared. Carnegie liked the gloss and used it as the title of his collected essays. I mention these elemental literary details because I would like to change the title again; I think my change might appeal to Mr. Carnegie's wraith which, if his jaded view of religion and his conception of earth as the only heaven turns out to be correct, may well be reading it. Carnegie was not an ordinary man, even in his generation. His ideas were quite stubbornly his own, and he kept a sometimes strange and unexpected control of what he wanted attributed to him.

I should like to call it "The Gospel of Wealth and Poverty," for it was the complex relation between the two that Carnegie saw more clearly than many in his generation. Indeed, if one goes back through the history of philanthropy as we understand it today, the intricate relation was what first distinguished philanthropy from charity for most of them and placed on philanthropy the responsibility for changing the conditions that made poverty possible. Carnegie had specifically rejected the glorification of the poor that had been one of the key doctrines of the Judeo-Christian tradition. Poverty taught important lessons to the poor, he thought, chief among them to search for the instruments that would lead the way out of it. It was the function of philanthropy to provide those instruments; and in "The Best Fields for Philanthropy" he described them.

His list was not likely to please the traditional dispensers of charity and Carnegie knew it. He placed churches last in his catalog of appropriate objects for philanthropy, just below swimming pools, and universities at the top, just above libraries. In the middle were meeting halls for public discussion and concerts. The search for knowledge pervaded his list and relaxation and the enjoyment of nature came next. Carnegie, more perhaps than any of the great philanthropists of his generation, was articulating a gospel that made science and technology the gods of his earthly heaven of wealth and nature the source and instrument of benevolence.

His attraction to Darwinism was really his discovery of a substitute for religion that would blend knowledge and nature to provide a leadership trained to create wealth as a byproduct of the blend. Using his own experience as his touchstone, he sought a system of education capable of making some among the poor as wealthy as he had become, those whose natural skills and energy enabled them to act as he had acted. But it would never include them all; and if his sense of the hierarchies of talent seems to us in conflict with his commitment to democracy, we must also measure them against our own accomplishments with poverty since.

Part of Carnegie's commitment came from his origins in a country that had turned its traditional fear of the poor into centuries of repressive legislation as far back as the reign of the first Elizabeth. Through the nineteenth century, reformers and legislators debated the choice between benevolence and imprisonment for those whose poverty led them into even minor crimes or whose financial misjudgments led them into debt. The Chartists, certainly among the most orderly of those seeking greater participation in government, were treated as dangerous disrupters of the public order and jailed for their audacity.

Although Tocqueville's descriptions of the way Americans dealt with such problems have an undoubtedly optimistic tone to them, the relatively limited character of American urban life, open lands, and chronic shortages of labor gave sufficient truth to the fabled land of opportunity to make the contrasts with Europe plausible. Carnegie's descriptions of his early years are probably accurate enough, while his mother's insistence on living in hotels that provided all of the services she had spent her young years struggling to produce for her family suggests a balance, perhaps, to his optimism. Not until after her death and his marriage late in life did Carnegie have a genuine home of his own. His mansion on Fifth Avenue and his recreation of a castle in Scotland were not allowed to be his first choices for himself, but he was finally able to carry them out on his own.

Most important is Carnegie's sense of the function of wealth in society and the role of those who control it. While his application of stewardship has strong roots in the Puritan conceptions voiced by men like John Winthrop, who helped provide North America with its first independently middle class settlements, there is in Carnegie's case a sense of management and skill born in the experience of the chaos of nineteenth century American growth and its costs to those who did not or could not make it. Part of his attraction to the Darwinian image, as he saw it, was his awareness of the fact that some of his contemporaries could use the materials presented them by the changing opportunities of American life, and some could not. While he could undoubtedly have been attracted to a Hegelian conception of leadership that tied the talents he sought to a culture he admired, American life, and his own life, had provided him no such model. Individual development through education, not the mystical growth of cultural giants, was the locus of achievement, and he directed his philanthropies toward the provision of the materials that would make that development possible.

His conviction that no man should die wealthy and his virtual contempt for inheritance as a way of attaining wealth give a rather hard reality to his conception of stewardship. More than any of the other giants of his generation he was convinced of the transience of life even amid the permanence of wealth, and his final philanthropic creation, the Carnegie Corporation of New York, confusing though its purposes may have been for those who continued to manage it, had none of his remaining family on its board. After his death Mrs. Carnegie's few requests were handled with all the courtesy and tact that can be summoned up by philanthropic managers committed to saying no. Her little handwritten notes were treated with gentle but unmistakable determination. His daughter, Margaret, was appointed to the board two decades after his death, but as a courtesy that was not extended to later descendants.

It even seems quite likely that the two men who did most to give the Corporation its present shape, Frederick Keppel and Henry

Pritchett, acted on their own in their establishment of the Corporation as an independent foundation rather than as a source of support for the other preexisting philanthropic enterprises Carnegie had created. Objections from men like Columbia's President, Nicholas Murray Butler, who felt certain they had heard the final plan from Mr. Carnegie's lips, moved them not at all. What they followed was a plan of stewardship that probably lay closer to Carnegie's heart than any of his lifetime suggestions. He had lived through a changing world he presumed would continue to change, and he rested his commitment to adjusting to change on the special strengths of a carefully selected staff.

With all of his Chartist sense of democracy, it is not easy to find a place for him in the American political movements of his day, perhaps because we have tended to define those movements in ways that exclude him. Although today's assessments of the Progressive movement have grown less respectful of the Progressives' willingness to accept cultural differences among the groups with whom they dealt, there is in the social reformers of the era a common belief that life did not have to be a struggle with intractable poverty, that the stages of development, as we would understand them today, could be happy and in tune with the natural world as they understood it. They revered family life, much as their critics today revere it. They sought ways of returning the young to the enriching environment of nature for the satisfactions and relaxation they saw there. Where their urban parks have not been desecrated by modern highway systems, they stand as monuments to that understanding. Conservation was a practice for them before it became a movement and the life cycle a reality they respected.

Carnegie's concern with retirement and old age were as much a part of his views of life as a whole as were his libraries and his gifts of barrels of his own Scotch whisky to American presidents. Yet it is unlikely that he will be credited with his larger views, despite "The Gospel of Wealth," or that the Progressives will get a better press among American historians, at least for the time being. The reason seems to me clear, now, but the answer to the questions it raises much less so.

No one, except possibly Carnegie, has attempted to define capitalism in a way which would invest it as an economic system with the morality and social responsibility Marx and Engels so forcefully sought to deny it. Thorstein Veblen has come as close to such a definition, I would argue, as any American theorist, but like many critics of capitalist irresponsibility—and like the brilliant satirist he was—Veblen so wonderfully defined the defects that he failed to support the virtues by anything other than the indirection that makes him the complex and difficult theorist he is.[7]

In Veblen's terms the profits of capitalism were misused when they were not invested in new production that could benefit both industry and society as a whole, but rather siphoned off for personal use which he called "conspicuous consumption." The Vanderbilts and their opulent estates were perfect examples of his criticism. Such large uses of wealth were, he thought, a drain on the system of production that made the success of capitalism possible in the first place. But, at least in his terms, the misuses were inherent not in the morality of capitalism but in the immorality of those who used it for such excessive personal benefit. It was a position the Puritans would have understood perfectly well, indeed, one they are sometimes credited with having invented.

Carnegie's capitalism is strikingly close to Veblen's. He sees it as a system that can, at its best, produce a vital process of the re-investment of the profits from production so as to expand future production, increase wages, satisfy consumer needs and desires, and leave still more surplus for the research into future innovations that will lead to further expansion of production. Herbert Hoover's ideal system, detailed in his autobiography but rarely read either by his supporters or his critics, argues exactly the same point.[8]

Carnegie's is close, even if it is crude by comparison, and his defenses of it clear in his writings. The Carnegie Institute in Pittsburgh, the Carnegie Institution in Washington, the libraries, the Hero Fund, the Endowment for International Peace, and indeed all of his philanthropies were designed to expand the range of opportunities available to those who could take advantage of them, and to increase the possibility of the taking of advantage by those who might otherwise have been dropped from the system. Even the simplified spelling he insisted on himself and forced his staff to use in their correspondence with others was an effort to make the learning and use of English easier for all to master.

The fact that neither he nor John D. Rockefeller chose to engage in welfare through their own industries to any great extent is evidence, I would argue, for their belief that the society needed a larger system of moral and social support than any one industry should be expected to supply. Their philanthropies were intended as an adjunct to capitalism, not an apology for it. The fact that they did not see government programs as the answer may be the result of a more complex problem that was based on the unwillingness of most Americans and most of their federal government to undertake such a responsibility, and the conviction on the part of many Americans that the inherent corruption of government would make any form of government welfare ineffective and wasteful.

The effort to produce a responsible capitalism that would not operate industry by industry, or business by business, or become a dependent upon government through taxation and the creation of public bureaucracies, led them, almost by inadvertence, to the creation of the system they initially established in their philanthropic corporations. The philanthropic system contained the morality and the social responsibility their corporate capitalism lacked, but it was clearly an adjunct to their corporate capitalism. What made it part of that corporate capitalism without subjecting it, in their terms, to any contradiction, was the fact that men like themselves could invest the system with their own morality and responsibility, and call upon others like themselves to do the same.

The paradox their system contained remains the paradox inherent in the philanthropic system we have inherited from them; and it is a paradox that puts us between the rock and the hard place of modern American society. Their system, and one sees it in Progressive reform as a whole, is built on a certitude by small groups of Americans of what all Americans need, a paternalism that rests inevitably on the choice by some of the directions that all are to follow. It is a problem that has made the Vanderbilt transformation of the private palace into public museum, a transformation similar to the choice made by John Paul Getty for the uses of his wealth after his death, much more viable than it has seemed to be for those attempting to broker a new philanthropy. Vanderbilt money did fund a university. Getty's did not. Getty's hostility to the very idea of philanthropy, and he made no bones about it, stands as a monument as significant in the world of philanthropy as his museum.

Although arguments about "tainted money" can be found in the initial era of modern philanthropy, there is a taint that appears at almost the same moment, one that is much harder to cope with, although, perhaps for that reason, less easily dealt with in open discussion. Organized modern philanthropy in its earliest years was designed to impress upon donees the judgments of the donor. The subsequent bureaucratization of the process through the emergence of the professional foundation manager has appeared to soften it somewhat without changing it. Carnegie's libraries required the financial support of the community in the form of a strict commitment to the purchase of books and library services. Rockefeller's remarkable gift to the University of Chicago required matching funds from the Chicago community.[9] Such gifts were intended to raise a philanthropic consciousness in the community, it was argued; but they also directed the consciousness it raised, placing behind it the authority of the donor's money as a significant force to fulfill the aims he had already determined to be good. The small communities that eagerly snapped up the offers of library buildings could find their own limited resources directed for an indefinite future toward aims they might not have agreed were the most essential, if, that is, they even bothered to debate those aims.

Carnegie was familiar not only with criticisms of his methods but the jokes it generated. At a Lotos Club dinner in his honor he listened to a fable of his ultimate trip to heaven where, at the Pearly Gates, St. Peter would send him back with half a halo, and the order to raise the money for the other half.[10] Chicago's Mr. Dooley played with the idea of the community's need for a library before anything else, toying somewhat more ironically with the whole notion. "Before another year," he wrote, "ivry house in Pittsburgh that ain't a blast furnace will be a Carnaygie libry. . . . I like him because he ain't shamed to give publicly," he went on. "Ye don't find him puttin' on false whiskers and turning up his coat-collar whin he goes out to be benivolent. No sir. Ivry time he dhrops a dollar it makes a noise like a waither fallin' down-stairs with a tray if dishes. He's givin' th' way we'd all like to give."[11]

There are significant figures in the American philanthropic world today who find matching funds a questionable focusing of a community's resources. There are others who consider Carnegie's kind of benevolence another form of demand on the community's limited

funds. At one major university where I once taught, the joke cir-
culated that if someone gave the university an elephant, it would
build an elephant house. More to the point, perhaps, Princeton
University has a lake of undoubted attractiveness but somewhat
questionable utility because that was what Mr. Carnegie told the
University's president, Woodrow Wilson, he thought the University
most needed from him. He had his purpose, and it wasn't land-
scaping. A lake would allow Princeton to introduce rowing crews
to replace football, a game he detested.[12]

In the early years of his pension fund gifts when Mr. Carnegie
controlled each benefaction, he would not give such a fund to a
college faculty of a sectarian school unless the college were willing
to sever its affiliation with its religious organization, thereby assuming for itself his own hostility to organized religion. Yet, he
manipulated state universities into asking for the funds themselves
lest he be accused in state legislatures of trying to influence state
educational policy. Mr. Carnegie's gifts were generous, but they
carried responsibilities that could themselves have costs. Whether
or not he chose to join them, and he apparently did not, he shared
with the Progressives of his generation what his parents shared with
the Chartists of their generation; that there was not only a need
for change but a direction it would best follow.

Lest an important point be lost, let me make it clear that no
one who has dealt with the government administrators in the federal
endowments and institutes that control funding for research has
any question that they, too, have strong senses of direction that
they are committed to following. Some of them are political. Some
are ideological. Some involve experiences with the disciplines represented in the administrative staffs, who see themselves not simply
as contributors to a process of research but participants in ways
their own talents may not have earned them. Although there were
moments back in the 1960s—when some of the federal organizations were first created—that some in the communities of academics
and artists who had been depending upon private funding felt
themselves released from directive controls they had sometimes
resented, government administrators showed themselves quick to
pick up the carrots they were dispensing and to see their magical
resemblance to sticks. Mr. Carnegie, certainly, would have had no
difficulty understanding their discovery and respecting it.

John Winthrop's conception of stewardship in his Model of Christian Charity is often where we begin our discussions of philanthropy. It establishes a sense of direction and purpose embodied in the steward himself. Both he and Andrew Carnegie understood the need to explain the predestination of some for wealth and others for poverty and to require the establishment of a relationship between them that placed a responsibility on the wealthy to contribute to the well-being of the poor. Both he and Andrew Carnegie understood that responsibility in fairly explicit terms: that there was a direction that improvement would best follow and toward which the steward was committed to leading. Although the two were more than two and a half centuries apart, the basic outlines of stewardship have remained remarkably unchanged. What has changed is the willingness of many in modern society to accept a single commitment as a given. We use the term "pluralism" to describe our sense of the many routes to many different conceptions of salvation; but we don't often acknowledge the mixed blessing it might be. The compromises it presses upon us diffuse resources when they are limited. Our experience with social reform, whether privately or publicly funded, has raised questions that make us less willing to look to money as the answer to all of our ills.

One can envy John Winthrop's certitude. The fact that it grew out of a society of believers who shared his understanding of an all powerful God that guided daily life, regardless of the predetermined decisions that set it on its course, makes it easier to understand not only his certainty but his joy in preaching it to a community prepared to accept any part of it they had not already been accustomed to believing. Winthrop had many tasks that would have tested most of us beyond endurance, but it seems likely that his belief in stewardship was not one of them. He and his followers expected an end to whatever doubts they may secretly have harbored when the return of Christ proved them right. They were sure it would be soon and they were more than willing to wait.

One can also admire Andrew Carnegie's certitude. And the more one knows of him, the more admirable, even audacious, it becomes. He seems not even to have shared his own community's religious commitments. His contributions of organs to churches he justified on the grounds that music conveyed more significant spiritual meanings than words. When asked to sell five acres of land to a Protestant cemetery, he replied, "I should be happy to present the land without price provided it were open to all who desired to rest there of every sect or of none. If you will make it free, a free resting place for every human being, Pagan, Christian or Jew, it will give me great pleasure to make the gift. We poor mortals while living our short span are far too sharply separated. Surely, we should not refuse to lie down together at last upon the bosom of mother earth."[13]

His comments on the names to be inscribed on the Carnegie Institute building in Pittsburgh—the closest we come to his convictions about art—are filled with fascinating outbursts: irritation that Scott was originally included rather than Burns, that Rubens was nothing more than a painter of fat women, that Raphael was just an imitator of his teacher, one could go on with critical commentary that has scarcely stood the test of time, although his musical taste seems to have been better.[14]

Such points are amusing, perhaps, but again beside the point. Carnegie's sense of stewardship was that of an American, not a transplanted English Puritan, and the difference is significant. He was not leading a society of the like minded but attempting to make a society of the like minded out of the chaos American society had become. An immigrant to the new world, he was building an even newer one inside it. Wealth was his tool. His confidence in his own judgment was his guide.

The question we need to ask is what kind of a conception of stewardship one can get out of such individualistic elements. Hoover saw the importance of individual judgment and the dangers of community coercion, as did Hoover's followers, but in an important sense and at an important moment in the history of modern philanthropy, the crisis of the Depression, Hoover seemed to fail. The tradition on which he tried to draw seemed to him to have been there, but it was gone. Roosevelt's compromises—the few that are still with us—are easily turned into models of discontent as one surveys the tradition now of farm subsidies and a social security program that looks sometimes like Dr. Seuss's Yertle the Turtle.

Another way of putting the question might be this: was the creation of the first foundations and the philanthropic activity they generated a unique moment in our history, the product of unique events in our national expansion and unique individuals who made decisions that are unlikely to be duplicated beyond the examples we are now familiar with, some of them just as remarkable as the initial ones. It was clear in the debate over the Tax Act of 1969 that those members of Congress who followed the notion that all foundations would have to declare themselves out of business forty years after their founding believed in some conception of uniqueness, or at least of a process that required being kept unique.

A contrasting way of putting the question would be this: did modern philanthropy create a method of social policy-making in American life that provides services that cannot be duplicated in our historic context by the centralizing process of policy-making our government has been undergoing since the Progressive era? I push it back that far to include the creation of the first big foundations as well as the first federal offices to deal with issues of the welfare of children and women, that is offices generated out of movement for social reform, many of them aided by research funded by the Russell Sage Foundation.

Despite all of our generalizations about the New Deal, it depended heavily on traditional private social agencies for its energy, just as Hoover had wanted government to. The various periods of expansion since that period, chiefly the Great Society, have uneasy support in the federal government, despite the great need for such support: and many of the crises faced by modern American society in fields like medical services are still built on efforts to bring private and public groups into working relationships that require money, to be sure, but new ideas above all, and committed intellects to produce them and to sustain them. People and ideas outside of the bureaucracies established to administer them have become the American protection against the anti-democratic tendencies inherent in all governments, democratic governments among them.

That last point is the issue that Carnegie saw, and Rockefeller along with him. It is the issue that so often seems missing from the debates about federal policy-making and local policy as well. What both men emphasized was the need to produce continuing generations of educated men and women capable not only of engaging in the process of problem solving but of producing in their turn new generations of men and women to continue their work— or, when necessary, to replace it. The essential difference between that concept of stewardship and John Winthrop's was the fact that the Puritan concept rested on an intervening God who seemed to them to promise an end to the process when the weary could rest and the rewards would be distributed. That may still come, as far as we know. Impatience would be foolish and disrespectful. But human life is short and those of us who are reluctant to waste even one such life may find ourselves in league with old Andrew.

One reason at least for my respect for him is the fact that our ability to produce destructive weapons and our need to open ourselves up to societies that are very different even from the communities he understood, let alone those John Winthrop led, place on us the responsibility of finding new ways to make the wealth we have work in our lifetimes for future benefit. Many of us don't have John Winthrop's understanding of what the future is going to be, but we are much more educated about our own lifetimes and much more able to make reasonable guesses about the future, what it will be if we participate in it, what it will be if we don't. Carnegie's sense of his present was like that. He loved life and the living and he committed himself to them.

Late in his life he wrote to a friend, "More and more I realize we should think less & less of 'Heaven our Home' and more & more of Home our Heaven. Wish I could get an option to leave this heaven only when I wisht."[15]

In keeping with that he turned his last hopes toward world peace, having created an institution devoted to that. Yet, he watched the coming of the First World War with the same practicality he had focused on everything else in his life and approved American entry in 1917. That was consistent with his understanding that future generations would manage his wealth better if he left them free to do it, and he did. So have they, as a matter of fact. We are forced to agree on the survival of that individual commitment to stewardship he left them. It may, in the long run, be his greatest gift.

The future is certainly less certain to us, even, than it was to him. His conviction that his money could bring an end to war seems to us simple and naive, particularly as we ponder the defense budget; but then a look at the costs of welfare is not likely to leave us any happier. What we can examine is his belief that responsibility for guiding the future was the ultimate human responsibility. It had to override gratification in the present. He saw no future beyond that, and his belief shaped everything he did.

That is, in some respects, the hardest of his convictions, that the only return he expected for his benevolence was the observation of the benevolence itself. He was buying no future reward and seeking expiation for no sins. Such a belief gives his philanthropy a hard reality that ties it irrevocably to life and the living. It gives his title, "The Gospel of Wealth," a realism we have to respect, whether or not we agree with it. In the last analysis, he understood what he was doing and why.

Notes

1. "In my young manhood we had everything to do and nothing to do it with; we had to hew our own paths along new lines; we had little experience to go on. Capital was most difficult to get, credits were mysterious things. Whereas now we have a system of commercial ratings, everything was then haphazard and we suffered from a stupendous war and all the disasters which followed." John D. Rockefeller, *Random Reminiscences of Men and Events* (1908–9; repr., Tarrytown, N.Y.: Sleepy Hollow Press and Rockefeller Archive Center, 1984), p. 14.

2. "For long years after, the head of this bank [from which Rockefeller received his first loan] was a friend indeed; he loaned me money when I needed it, and I needed it almost all the time and all the money he had. . . . It is a pleasure to testify even at this late date to his great kindness and faith in me." Ibid., p. 48.

3. "We never attempted . . . to sell Standard Oil stock on the market through the Stock Exchange. In the early days the risks of the business were great, and if the stock had been dealt in on the Exchange its fluctuations would no doubt have been violent. We preferred to have the attention of the owners and administrators of the business directed wholly to the legitimate development of the enterprise rather than to speculation in its shares." Ibid., p. 65–66.

4. That quotation and the Carnegie motto on the escutcheon he designed as the family coat of arms, "Death to Privilege," are used by Wall as introductory mottos for his biography. Joseph Frazier Wall, *Andrew Carnegie* (New York, 1970), p. 2.

5. The remark by Colonel E. L. Drake is quoted in a memoir by Edward Harkness in the Commonwealth Fund papers, Rockefeller Archives. Rockefeller began his explorations in Drake's Pennsylvania.

6. See the biography of Andrew Mellon by Allen Nevins in the *Dictionary of American Biography*.

7. It may be characteristic of Veblen that the best explanations of his relation to capitalist theory are by his students. I am thinking most of Wesley Clair Mitchell's introduction to his collection of readings from Veblen, "What Veblen Taught."

8. *The Memoirs of Herbert Hoover*, volume 2 (New York, 1952). On

pages 28 and 29 Hoover lists his answers to the problems of industrial
instability.

9. The most sensitive history of the early years of the University of
Chicago remains that of Thomas W. Goodspeed, *The History of the University of Chicago* (Chicago, 1916).

10. Henry S. Pritchett at the dinner to Andrew Carnegie, March 17,
1909. *After Dinner Speeches at the Lotos Club* (New York, 1911), p. 419.

11. "The Carnegie Libraries," pp. 177–182 in *Dissertations by Mr.
Dooley* (New York, 1906).

12. Wall, p. 868.

13. Wall, p. 1009.

14. Wall, p. 817.

15. Wall, p. 1009.

Aristotle and the Ethics of Philanthropy

ALBERT ANDERSON

Are the wealthy obliged by virtue of their status to be philanthropic? The idea that with wealth go responsibilities, particularly for a "public good" that is responsive to charitable causes, is an old one. In the Judeo-Christian tradition it follows from the maxim, "To whom much is given will much be required."[1] How much is not always clear except perhaps in the New Testament story of the rich man who was challenged by Jesus to give it *all* away in preparation for life in heaven. That the rich man could not bring himself to do it, eliciting Jesus' comment that it is easier for a camel to pass through the eye of a needle, no doubt addresses the order of life's priorities.[2] It also dramatically underscores a sense of duty to be altruistic that, as Immanuel Kant, the great eighteenth-century philosopher, would say, is likely to be at odds with human disposition.

If the wealthy have responsibilities by virtue of their lot, then few writers make any stronger case for the claim than Aristotle, prior to the Christian era, in his classic *Nichomachean Ethics*. Indeed, the case is more intriguing because of the widespread and ethically limited use of the concept of responsibility. Aristotle's words are paraphrased by modern-day professionals in philanthropy as: "To give away money is an easy matter, and in everyone's power. But to decide to whom to give it, and how large, and for what purpose is neither in everyone's power nor an easy matter."[3]

No doubt the professionals, and I am one, adorn their walls with the paraphrase for its enduring applicability—and respectability. To fund raisers whose art and profession it is to solicit charitable gifts for worthy causes, it may suggest the difficulty in making an effective case to a prospective donor. To grantmakers whose job it is to steward and distribute the funds entrusted to them, it represents the complex decision-making inherent in giving limitedresources to only a few.

Clearly, Aristotle's words serve a dual purpose to express their respective roles for mastering the arts of raising and distributing funds for worthy causes. But his sense of "responsible" wealth is more profound and complex, and clarifying the concept of responsibility by distinguishing its various uses is critical. A personal experience may serve to provide the context.

I. A Lesson in Philanthropy: Part One

Some years ago, as a rookie private college president anxious to strengthen the business program there, I determined to make a call on a wealthy prospect, the CEO of a family-owned business whose product was distributed worldwide. To lend maximum clout to the request, I asked a longtime, generous college donor to accompany me. Equally wealthy, he was the CEO of an industry competitor, also family-owned. Needless to say, it was not a call he enjoyed making. But for my request he would never have set foot in that office. Knowing how much we needed the funds, he agreed to come along for support and attest to how it could strengthen the business department, an area of obvious common interest. In the course of the visit we asked for a substantial gift to endow annual public symposia featuring eminent speakers to address the issues and interrelationships of business, ethics, and the liberal arts.

The prospect warmed to the idea—so much so that, having made up his mind later to do it, he initiated very similar offers to at least two other colleges. (Judging from our discussion, he may have reasoned that a friendly "competition" among area colleges would follow, a situation not unlike the American free enterprise system in which competitive markets contribute to a healthy economic climate of quality products at fair prices.)

But he had some conditions in mind. The program would carry the donor's name—a possibility I may have quite innocently suggested as an appropriate means of donor recognition, but which I now sensed would amount to company advertising worth several times the value of the grant; the program would be on trial for three years, at which time the donor might withdraw the gift if he felt the program did not prove to be effective; and its aim should be to promote "the free enterprise system."

I had been naive, outsmarted, not suspecting that in reality the prospect and I were not talking about a "gift." Instead, we were negotiating a mutually beneficial arrangement of services for funds—in economic terms, an "exchange of values."

I realized too late that there were a lot of things I should have been prepared to say. However, the best I could do at the moment was to pick up on the one condition that as president I could not live with: the promise to showcase a particular set of values to the exclusion of the broad and often conflicting values which are daily examined (and debated to no consensus) in a liberal arts setting.

In short, I tried to elicit from the wealthy prospect the willingness to create a forum for free enterprise advocates and critics alike. But that, I sensed, was a concession he was unwilling to make. At the risk of seeming condescending I wanted to ask him what he meant by "free enterprise system." I knew it would not do to put him on the defensive and expose even deeper differences between his world and mine. I hoped he might leave enough latitude in the concept to include both its uses and its abuses, its strengths and weaknesses. In that case I could promote it in good conscience, and with the confidence that it had a fair chance to succeed over the length of the offer.

My attempt was impotent. He was an eloquent advocate of "the system" who clearly felt that when applied with requisite skill, it had no weaknesses and certainly no ethical limitations. He argued that free enterprise gets a "bad rap" from the media-led public, and especially from academics, even business professors who are practically ignorant of the business world ("they've never had to make a payroll!"). They are unappreciative of the good things that the system does for them and hindered by their ivory towers from recognizing the complexities and difficulties of the real world.

It was a classic rejoinder, and the point of departure for a grand but wholly imprudent, if not futile, debate. I had no idea how to proceed. What responsibilities had I as a fund raiser, and he as a donor, overlooked?

II. Responsible Wealth

In a common sense of the term, to be responsible is to be the *cause* of something. Ordinarily the fact that a wealthy donor is the agent of a gift is a necessary, but not a sufficient, condition of responsible action.

Typically, the wealthy quite freely assume a *role*—responsibility in a second sense of the term—to do what only they can substantially do. Playing various roles is generally serious business for all of us. As a parent, or citizen, or board member, or professional, we are conscious of a particular job description. We define the aims and expectations peculiar to each role, and delineate and assume them as "responsibilities."

Responsibility in this second sense is derivative, justified by reference to the job to be done, the mission of the organization, or the objective of the donor. And as we shall see, this sense is especially important for understanding the normative force of "codes of ethics."

Suppose the wealthy do come to regard themselves as, in the first sense, having caused or contributed to the problem? Or suppose they subscribe to the scriptural principle that to whom much is given much will be required? Then a third—and *moral*—sense of responsibility is at stake.

Moral responsibility, according to Aristotle, typically depends on motives governed by principles.[4] If I seek through a generous gift to redress a wrong I caused, I act out of a sense of *justice,* not out of generosity. Generosity, or better, beneficence, becomes an accompanying consideration—a consequence—not the governing principle. Both are morally grounded, but one is preeminent. Thus, it would better serve the notion of responsible wealth if beneficence *per se* was the prior principle.

The governing principle is important. There are some professionals for whom the gift is everything, and the source or motive behind it is not a philanthropic concern. If philanthropy is defined by the good it does, then the founder of The Salvation Army was right; he reputedly said, "I would take money from the devil himself and wash it in the tears of the widows and little children." The argument that a good cause can clean up "dirty money" is attractive, but it hardly makes the devil a philanthropist. What is a gift? Is there no reason to blanch at a grant from a Boesky-like source? Or are the cynics right who say it is the *amount* that creates the scruples?

Recently a university foundation received a major sum from a convicted bid rigger, an amount ordered and designated by the trial judge "to be used by the department of philosophy with particular reference to the study of ethics as it pertains to business practices in the State and the United States." The department will use the money as the judge requires; however, it is not a "gift." From Aristotle's perspective, neither the bid rigger nor the judge, however well disposed he is to encourage ethical behavior, is a philanthropist.

III. The Philanthropic Virtue

There is no question but that the wealthy can and do assume the philanthropic role, and fund raisers and grantmakers have a legal and fiduciary responsibility to carry out philanthropists' intentions. But Aristotle's position is more intriguing: the wealthy also have a moral responsibility for *being* philanthropic.

Better than most, Aristotle understood the difference between responsibility as a role we assume, and responsibility as a principle of human behavior—an *enduring disposition* which evolves as moral "character."[5] Grounded in character, the capacity for uncommon beneficence is wedded to the need for what is ethically right and good. Disposed by good choices, character yields liberality (beneficence), the philanthropic virtue, one of a select number of lifestyle components that, according to Aristotle, accrue both to be the individual's and the community's "well being."

Aristotle was a teleologist. He believed we seek our own greatest happiness, an end for which everything else is a means. This is not, however, the simple notion that the end justifies the means, nor an ancient form of utilitarianism. It is a kind of human self-realization in which the means chosen to achieve good ends should be good as well.

In Aristotle's view, moral responsibility is a matter of character development, not so much a solitary act of goodness as a *readiness* always to act in the most virtuous or morally excellent manner.

Achieving moral excellence, in turn, begins as a natural bent to gain happiness mainly by discovering a pattern of actions shaped by self-conscious choices that "draw the line" between too much and too little, the excessive and the deficient—hardly, as the Aristotle paraphrase insists, "an easy matter." Drawing lines is probably the earliest and most enduring metaphor of ethics. To Aristotle, while ethics clearly offers no science of Euclidean-like truths, it is nonetheless a demanding and thoroughly rational art, whose mastery is vital to the well being of human nature.

Indeed, as Aristotle understood it, the philanthropic virtue exemplified this task by requiring that two of the arts we most admire—that of acquiring wealth and that of distributing it—be combined, *with integrity,* in one and the same concept.

That is, the true philanthropist somehow combines both arts without conflict of reason, interest, or value, though each is conceptually distinct, governed by quite different skills, ends, and means. If to be philanthropic is an enduring aspect of one's behavior and not a label we fix on discrete acts of generosity, then it must be possible both to give and to get, to distribute wealth and to replace it again, in order to repeat the process with regularity as one expression of the virtuous life.

As the opening paraphrase says, that is "neither in everyone's power nor an easy matter": one cannot continue to distribute wealth without replacing it; yet the task is to ensure that each part of the interrelationship is done in the most admirable way. And that is the moral arena in which those who claim the right to be philanthropic must compete.

Perhaps in this Aristotle and Jesus agree: the rich man has a harder time of it than the camel. But what is so hard?

IV. Professional Responsibility

Setting aside the first, or causal, use of responsibility, we can begin to understand the difficulty by distinguishing between one's professional, social, or cultural role and one's moral obligation. For one who has the resources to give, the *role* is, as Aristotle says, relatively easy to play. Giving, however, is *morally* appropriate only when both means and ends are sought and served by well-guided character.

The distinction is important. Role responsibility is basic to the nature of what we today regard as "codes of ethics." No doubt Aristotle would affirm the need and usefulness of professional and business codes. Indeed, President Bush has made the development of a new code governing the conduct of public servants a national priority, and has declared that "apparent conflict of interest," a typical emphasis in business and professional codes, should be its guiding principle.[6]

In the context of influence peddling, cover-ups, and deception of Congress under oath, not to mention insider trading, genetic engineering, and breach of privacy, there is good reason to attend to codes of conduct in all sectors of society. Like a network of limited "social contracts," these codes are both implicit and explicit. They are part of the pluralistic, patchwork fabric of personal commitments that hold contemporary American society together.[7]

The seduction is that codes have the look, but not the substance, of moral principle, and thus they tempt one to substitute the provisions of the codes for the character that justifies them—a mistake that Aristotle would not make.

Departing somewhat from the letter but not the spirit of Aristotle, let me suggest that by their very nature codes have two major shortcomings: first, as standards of ethical conduct, they are not self-justifying; and second, as guides to practical action, they are not self-clarifying.

Briefly, a code is a set of values shared by a group, stemming from a common interest, objective, or role. By assuming the role, one assumes the responsibilities it entails, particularly in relation to those individuals and groups who have a stake in the purposes of the role. In short, the code responsibilities derive their authority from the group's *raison d'être*.

However, we do not assume that because the Mafia has a code, its norms are ethically appropriate. That will not be so until they are justified by more fundamental, generally durable principles, such as truth-telling, promise-keeping, respect for individual rights, and the like.

Thus the idea is to develop provisions or normative generalizations that can be justified by the most basic ethical principles. Even so, they are only generalizations, static but open-ended guides for organizing the dynamic, complex, day-to-day experiences of choosing morally specific actions. As one who looks to a code for guidance knows, the norms are not self-clarifying, short of the situations that refine and make them meaningful.

Codes also have two important advantages. In the first place, they help us identify and safeguard certain interests or "values" of the individual, the group, and others including the public at large who have a stake in our proposes. In the rather simplistic sense suggested by the President, this process defines ethics itself, seen by some as the locus for "conflict of values." For this reason, codes give major attention to actual and potential conflicts of interest, which can be very subtle. "Apparent" conflict is used well if it suggests the need to erase suspicion; if the charge is politically motivated, however, the intention may be merely mischievous.

In fact, in the second place, codes are intended to elicit trust. The governing ethical principle *implicit* in virtually every code is integrity: neither the individual nor the public at large can have confidence in a group whose norms are inconsistently or hypocritically exemplified. The code is a public test of the organization's declaration of responsibilities.

Aristotle's point is simple but fundamental: being a responsible professional in philanthropy is not the same as being a morally responsible philanthropist.

V. The Well-Motivated Philanthropist

To Aristotle, the person we universally admire is always drawing lines, consistently discerning and embodying behavior that is just right. Such constancy arises out of and builds on character. Together with justice (temperance)—the only other distinctively *moral* virtue—philanthropy is fundamental to human well being. The morally excellent person will be liberally disposed, one who embodies that famous "golden mean" between the vice-prone extremes of extravagant spending and Scrooge-like behavior.

That is only one side of it. How one acquires wealth is closely related to how one gives it away, and the rightness of governing motives is critical. While it is true that wealth is a necessary condition for philanthropy, it is not sufficient. The idea of a well-motivated philanthropist whose wealth is gained by consciously fraudulent or harmful means is an oxymoron.

While Aristotle does allow in his *Ethics* for harmful actions that are done involuntarily or out of ignorance, the correcting of those actions through charity would not qualify as philanthropic. An act must be voluntary to be either praiseworthy or blameworthy, and unless the governing motive is to be charitable, it is not philanthropic.

A recent case involving a private college is instructive.[8] In response to a major capital gift, the college publicly announced that it would name a new building after the donor. Shortly afterward it was discovered and widely reported that for years the donor had carried out an extensive one-man crusade, anonymously by mail, against what he regarded as the evils of interracial and mixed-religious marriages. Recipients of his letters felt frightened and harassed. When confronted, he insisted that he had meant no harm, and that, based on his reading of the Old Testament, his only intention was to educate such persons to the dangers of their new relationships. To the embarrassment of the college, a church-related, liberal arts institution, the contrast between its mission and his was stark. The college, which had already committed the funds, decided to keep the gift but remove his name from the building—conditions the donor agreed to. Question: Is the donor a philanthropist? And is it the gift or the thought "that counts"?

For Aristotle, both the gift and the thought are important. Unfortunately, the widow's mite, for all its magnitude relative to her resources, will not qualify. Only a gift that measurably enhances the public good will do. However, the donor's governing motive for giving—what we today call "the charitable intent"—is paramount, because it is fundamental to character. Charitable intent implies the donor is disposed to be beneficent and expects nothing but a sense of well being in return. No *quid pro quo* results in personal influence or economic advantage. Moreover, charitable intent does not end with the donor. Its virtue is cultivated and developed by an ethical fund raiser or recipient organization that takes care to avoid misleading requests for funds.

Sometimes, however, *quid pro quo* arrangements can be very subtle. In recent years development professionals have couched their fund raising efforts in marketing terms. To avoid any sense of crassness, we speak of "an exchange of values" (not necessarily ethical values) that takes place between the donor and recipient organization. While the concept is very effective for promoting the relationship, it tends to focus unduly on businesslike transactions that appeal to the smart consumer, well short of the idea of charitable intent.

In the case of the liberal arts college, the obvious clash with a moderately Judeo-Christian reading of the Old Testament was not the donor's governing reason, or he would have withdrawn the gift once the difference with his own views became clear. Perhaps it was simply the educational mission of the college, the tradition of free inquiry and open debate, that moved him to give. (Ostensibly, by taking the gift the college saw no conflict between its *confessional* heritage and its educational nature.)

Or was he, based on his personal financial planning, simply sold on the prospect of substantial tax savings? The strategy is not lost on fund raisers, either. The competition for charitable dollars prompts nonprofit organizations to more aggressively market planned gifts as prudent, wealth-*conserving* proposals to prospective donors.

To Aristotle, the charitable intent makes a difference to moral character. Today, however, there are those who hold that except for illegal or unreasonable restrictions on a gift, a donor's motives are not relevant to the definition of philanthropy. A donor, we argue, may have multiple motives, impossible to prioritize, let alone detect. It is absurd to think that nonprofit organizations such as hospitals, churches, and colleges should accept money only from the pure of heart.

But assume that the college donor intended his gift as a gift, with no strings attached. Is there any reason *not* to regard him as a philanthropist? Only if one presses the case that he was deluded, which relieves him of culpability and thus of moral blame. On the surface his personal vision was not based on poor observation or faulty logic. On the contrary, he went about his educational mission self-consciously, if insensitively, and true to his convictions. His intentions were as honorable as the source of his wealth.

Yet it is difficult to avoid the criticism that the college had taken "dirty money," with which philanthropy should not be associated. For example, it has been said that by accepting the gift from one of such shocking convictions the college not only is sending out messages that seem contrary to its mission, it is also "debasing public standards."

It is one thing to require that philanthropic wealth originate on ethical grounds. Does it also require that its *recipients* be ethical?

Aristotle would not likely relieve the recipient organization or fund raiser of moral responsibility. He would probably regard the advent of professional fund raisers and grantmakers as agents and champions of philanthropic virtue, representing both of its major components: rightly gaining and distributing wealth.

In this more complex society, moreover, he would have expected them to be specialists in charitable intent, and to abide by morally justifiable codes which require that gifts, particularly those designated by the donor, clearly be encouraged and solicited *as* gifts, to serve the organization's mission and objectives without conflict of values.

Again, few authors would surpass Aristotle in his sensitivity to "public standards," whatever that means, given his view that the ultimate purpose of philanthropy is to enhance "the public good" by ethical means. In the case of the college donor, we have no reason to suspect an unethical source of wealth—not at least to the degree we suspect it among those we classically identify with the history of American philanthropy.

Do we debase public standards by taking money from the Rockefellers and Carnegies of this nation? Or does the good they have done make up for the bad that may have led to their wealth? Perhaps it is enough to concede that modern-day organized philanthropy follows hard on the heels of wealth gained at the expense of human life, destruction of the environment, and harm to the health and well being of untold numbers of people. No doubt by utilitarian standards the economic impact those great leaders of industry and finance made on the nation has been for the public good.

However, a cost/benefit analysis of the trade-off is absurd, unless human life and dignity have a purely economic value. Although Aristotle might have commended John D. Rockefeller for his sense of justice in establishing a foundation to compensate for the killing of innocent children at his mine in Colorado, the action could not justify the means, nor qualify as philanthropic.

Nonetheless, while philanthropy may have been born of questionable lineage, it has long since transcended the means by which its original character was imprinted. If the good has made up for the bad, that is only fair, a matter of justice, but not a matter of philanthropy. Each is determined on its own merits. Classical philanthropy today is both honorable and impressive.

VI. The Complete Philanthropist

While the ideal of philanthropy is to be virtuous both in making and distributing one's wealth, Aristotle, like Jesus, subscribed to the notion that it is more blessed to give than to receive. True, we admire the person with the Midas touch, but it is not morally admirable in the absence of a disposition to be generous.

To Aristotle, there is an interrelationship: it is better to perform good actions than to refrain from bad ones—which together with being generous makes a good philanthropist. While avoiding harm strikes us as an important, even guiding, ethical principle in America today, it is a weak substitute for well-grounded freedom of choice and action. The point applies to both the giver and the fund raiser: the idea is regularly to acquire wealth by actively ethical means and distribute it well. In their giving, Aristotle suggests, philanthropists will seek no favors designed to increase their wealth. They should in this respect sharply separate how they give from how they acquire. To confuse one's talent for making money, which may be good and honorable, with the talent for giving it away is a deception. To combine them, each with its own integrity, is the art of philanthropy.

The fundamental role philanthropists play is to maximize the public good by carrying out an "excellent" objective. As the opening paraphrase of Aristotle suggests, the challenge is to give generously to the "right persons," presumably virtuous, admirable leaders; in the "right amount," that is, a balance of one's means and the end they can serve; and at the "right time," whenever the need coincides with what can be accomplished. The grantmakers of this nation appreciate the challenge of defining such aims, whenever they stand by their stated purposes, do not presume too much in deciding what is good for society, and minimize the occasional whimsy or favorite causes of powerful board members.

The temptation is to find contemporaries who approach Aristotle's ideal. The example of Stewart Mott, of the family that established the Mott Foundation, is interesting. Heir to millions of his own, as a young man he assumed the role of professional philanthropist differently from that of his family. Conscious of a personal responsibility to address the concerns of his "boomer" generation for the future, he continues to direct his own resources and those he raises to such causes as peace, population control, honest government, civil liberties, and women's rights—causes he feels are vital to society.[9]

Stewart Mott is wealthy by certain standards, but the meaning of wealth is vague. To be a millionaire, let alone give a million dollars, is hardly extraordinary today. If wealth is relative, defined as a surplus of resources over needs, it would seem to follow that the proverbial widow who gave her mite also qualifies as a philanthropist. As we noted earlier, however, the impact of the gift is questionable. Given his penchant for proportion, Aristotle probably would be more inclined to qualify her as a philanthropist if her mite buys a loaf of bread that saves a life than if it is added to the major gifts needed to construct a shipyard for trade with other countries.

To Aristotle, the impact of the gift is important. He imposes a special obligation on the very wealthy who can make a truly "magnificent" gift. To embody magnificence, which avoids the extremes of vulgarity and shabbiness, requires that one focus the gift specifically on the betterment or welfare of the community, a concept which for Aristotle has the force of "nation."

In return, the donor may expect to experience the pleasure that comes both from benefiting society and from satisfying the moral responsibilities of wealth.

VII. A Lesson in Philanthropy: Part Two

According to Aristotle, moral excellence is first and foremost a dispositional, attitudinal characteristic of the individual. It is the acknowledgment that I am faced with a responsibility to do what is right and good for its own sake. It calls upon my character, not simply the role I am socially expected to play by virtue of being a professional or a parent or a member of the corporate community.

To Aristotle, there is a right and wrong way to get and to give. Some may argue that how a donor made his wealth is irrelevant; it is the gift that counts. Not quite, says Aristotle. Being philanthropic is an enduring trait of character, not a one-time act, and no giving done at the price of dishonesty can possibly be admired by the recipient or bring true pleasure to the donor. The virtuous philanthropist will regularly acquire, distribute, and replace wealth rightly, only to distribute it well again.

The end of the story of my experience as a young college president asking for a major gift from a wealthy but business-minded prospect, with the aid of an equally wealthy but other-minded donor, may serve to confirm the enduring value of Aristotle's insights into the ethics of philanthropy. Ineffective in eliciting either the prospect's understanding of the college's purposes or his charitable intent, I had no idea how, in the best interests of philanthropy, to continue the discussion.

Fortunately I did not have to go on. My wealthy donor colleague did it for me. In a tone revealing his impatience, he began by challenging his competitor to match his own long-standing advocacy of the free enterprise system, a fact I am certain my proud prospect must have counted on to strengthen, not weaken, his grant conditions. The opening established the parity of their credentials and nicely leveled the playing field. My volunteer partner went on to say he had no reservations about examining the American economic system from various perspectives and in fact was confident that its principles and practices were sound enough to withstand public criticism.

But what galled him most, he continued, was that anyone would presume to put any condition whatsoever on a gift. He himself had given millions of dollars over the years to the college, never once extracting a condition. In essence he said, "You know very well that if you have confidence in the place, especially in its leadership, you shouldn't have a problem about giving. If they say they need something, it's only a matter of deciding what you can do to make it happen. What would this community be without the college? You've got the money; we both believe in good business education; you can support this program without the slightest reservation!"

For all practical purposes the visit came to an end without a decision from the prospect. Some time later I received a letter from him informing me of the grant, with only the naming and probationary conditions still there. After explaining to my governing board what had happened, we accepted it in the confidence that a successful program would result in a permanent addition to the college's endowment.

In the context of Aristotle's case for philanthropic virtue, the lessons of this experience probably require no further analysis. In simple but profound terms, the wealthy donor who accompanied me on that visit, and whom I learned to admire for his eminently successful and humane business practices, exemplifies to this day what Aristotle meant by philanthropy and the responsibilities of wealth.

Notes

1. Luke 12:48.
2. Matthew 19:16–24.
3. Actually a paraphrase culled from Chapters 1 and 2, Book IV, *The Nichomachean Ethics,* many translations.
4. Cf. ibid., Books II and III.
5. Cf. ibid., Book I.
6. In a speech to high-level federal officials January 25, 1989, reported by Christopher Matthews, *San Francisco Examiner.*
7. The analogy of a code of ethics with a social contract warrants a separate discussion. The nature of the social contract and its ethical underpinnings in American society is thoroughly examined in *Habits of the Heart,* by Robert N. Bellah, Richard Madsen, William M. Sullivan, Ann Swidler, and Steven M. Tipton (New York: Harper & Row, 1985).
8. Cf. the article by Jeremy Iggers in the Minneapolis–St. Paul *Star Tribune,* March 6, 1988.
9. Vance Packard, in an excerpt from his book, *The Ultra Rich: How Much Is Too Much?* (Boston: Little, Brown & Co., 1989), carried by the *Star Tribune* newspaper.

Philanthropy under _Capitalism_

JONATHAN RILEY

"But sometimes Virtue starves, while Vice is fed."
What then? Is the reward of Virtue bread?
   . . . . . .
Know then this truth (enough for Man to know)
"Virtue alone is happiness below."

—Alexander Pope
An Essay on Man, Epistle IV,
lines 149–50, 309–10.

American philanthropy is usually held to be distinctive despite its old world heritage. Daniel Boorstin pursues this line of thought, for example, by pointing to at least three peculiar aspects of the American philanthropic spirit: its concern for the character of the recipient, not that of the giver; its focus on solving problems in this life, not on saving souls for the next; and its preoccupation with uplifting the community, not palliating the conscience. Those peculiarities may be taken to illustrate an idealistic kind of individualism that underpins the traditional American notion of community:

> A wise act of philanthropy would sooner or later benefit the giver along with all other members of the community. . . . Just as the value of a charitable gift tended to be judged less by the motive of the giver than by the social effect of the gift, so the suitability of a recipient was judged less by his emotional response—his gratitude or his personal loyalty to a benefactor—than by his own potential contribution to the community.[1]

More generally, Merle Curti suggests that "philanthropy has both reflected and helped create an American middle way between a type of capitalism characteristic of the old world, in which owners surrender little of what they have unless forced to do so, on the one hand, and socialism on the other."[2] Put in other words, American philanthropy affirms a distinctive conception of moral virtue that suitably constrains both capitalism and democratic government for the good of the community.[3]

Nevertheless, philanthropy, with its "middle way" between crude materialistic individualism and coercive state socialism, continues to face major challenges from both the left and the right in the United States.[4] Those challenges are in large part tied up with the idiosyncratic development of American federalism, in particular the changing role of the national government.[5] Many critics see philanthropy as merely a temporary handmaiden for the late-emerging national welfare state, whereas some putative defenders seem to assume that more unrestrained capitalism will automatically generate sufficient philanthropy to replace any federal cutbacks in social programs. In any case, the boundaries among capitalism, philanthropy, and democratic government have become increasingly blurred, raising serious doubts that philanthropy is really all that distinctive an activity anyway.[6]

My main theme is that philanthropy in America celebrates a certain liberal conception of moral virtue whose role in the preservation and operation of the American polity is not sufficiently appreciated. I am not suggesting that all strands of American philanthropy are liberal in this sense. Nor do I mean to deny that philanthropic practices under capitalism have evolved from earlier religious practices. Perhaps a persuasive case can be made, for example, that the calculating spirit of liberal philanthropy evolved in Weber-like fashion from the Protestant Ethic.[7] Nevertheless, whatever we make of the argument that aspirations to do good for others are rooted in certain religious traditions, it remains convenient to distinguish liberal from non-liberal philanthropy. At the risk of oversimplification, non-liberal philanthropy rests on a personal devotion to authority, for example, the will of god or the opinion of a majority. The right motivation, the wish to help others, is sufficient for charity and moral virtue on this view. No attempt rationally to assess the consequences of one's giving is necessary. Beneficence is reduced to benevolence. Charity is simply a matter of being disposed to help, without question, in accord with existing social and religious customs. Doing good becomes equivalent to *wishing* to do as authority dictates, nothing more.

Liberal philanthropy, in contrast, holds that the wish to help others may be necessary but is certainly not sufficient for authentic charity and moral virtue. Doing good also requires a warranted belief that the effects of one's giving will be beneficial to the community. Rational assessment of the consequences of the gift is necessary, particularly of its effects on the characters of the recipients. Unwise gifts that actually do more harm than good by encouraging idleness and undue dependence, for example, are *not* philanthropic even though well-intentioned. In Benjamin Franklin's words: "Liberality is not giving much but giving wisely."[8] Thus, liberal moral virtue demands not merely a benevolent disposition but also an intellectual capacity to discern the probable consequences of giving, with a view to evaluating and perhaps modifying existing social conventions relating to charity. In short, the existing conventions may be unfit as means, and should be open to reform through free discussion, education and persuasion.[9]

To begin to clarify the importance of this latter kind of philanthropy for the liberal polity in theory and for the American polity in practice, I propose to reconsider Andrew Carnegie's so-called "Gospel of Wealth."[10] Whatever we may think of Carnegie the man, there is little doubt that this gospel influenced significantly the shape not only of his own life but also that of American capitalism.[11]

I. Carnegie's Gospel of Wealth

"The fundamental idea" of the gospel of wealth is that "surplus wealth should be considered as a sacred trust to be administered by those into whose hands it falls, during their lives, for the good of the community."[12] By surplus wealth, Carnegie appears to mean wealth that legitimately accrues to an individual as a result of his property rights but which is beyond the needs of his family and not otherwise invested in real plant and equipment. Family needs are to be determined according to tacit community standards: "There must be different standards for different communities."[13]

Essentially, the rule is to avoid offending middle class customs through ostentatious living: "Whatever makes one conspicuous offends the canon."[14] Capital goods are exempt from redistribution because wealth in this form is not available for personal use. Such wealth is already engaged in "beneficent wonders," that is, "enterprises which give employment and develop the resources of the world." Surplus wealth, by contrast, apparently consists of idle assets like cash, stocks, and bonds that people hoard beyond their needs in banks and elsewhere, "adding the interest . . . to the principal, and [perhaps] dying with their treasures 'laid up,' which should have been used as they accrued during the life of the individual for public ends, as the gospel of wealth requires."[15]

Although the notion of surplus wealth remains a bit unclear, Carnegie's gospel suggests two main ethical principles for guiding the practice of philanthropy under capitalism. First, wealthy individuals have a moral obligation to distribute their surplus wealth for beneficial public purposes such as the provision of higher education. That obligation to the community apparently supersedes legal property rights, despite Carnegie's view that "upon the sacredness of property civilization itself depends—the right of the laborer to his hundred dollars in the savings-bank, and equally the legal right of the millionaire to his millions."[16] Second, the wealthy are also obligated to administer the distribution of wealth themselves during their own lifetime. That responsibility cannot be discharged through bequests. And it is positively at odds with any claim that governments, democratic or otherwise, should be solely responsible for the provision of public goods.[17] Instead, it requires any individual blessed with unusual riches to become an unusual kind of leader in his community, that is, a leader whose activities are not necessarily approved by government officials. The wealthy person has a duty to sponsor projects that *he* has reason to believe will actually benefit his fellows: "the surplus which accrues from time to time in the hands of a man should be administered by him in his own lifetime for that purpose which is seen by him, as trustee, to be best for the good of the people. To leave at death what he cannot take away, and place upon others the burden of the work which it was his own duty to perform, is to do nothing worthy. This requires no sacrifice, nor any sense of duty to his fellows."[18]

Active participation by the wealthy in community affairs distinguishes the liberal kind of philanthropy exemplified by Carnegie's own life.[19]

It is worth emphasizing that Carnegie's two principles apply to *personal* holdings of wealth. Individual owners are called upon to give money and time for the benefit of the community. Thus, the gospel of wealth remains as relevant today as in 1889. Its prescriptions do not depend on the structure of the capitalist economy. That the American economy today is dominated by large-scale multinational corporations rather than by small-scale competitive enterprises simply does not matter. Moreover, despite the modern legal fiction that a corporation is a person, the gospel of wealth does not extend without caveat to corporate philanthropy. In particular, corporate managers have no justification for distributing profits to community projects without permission from a majority of shareholders. Instead, the focus is on the owners of the company to distribute their dividends for worthwhile community causes. Even if shareholders consent to distribute their surplus wealth jointly rather than as separate individuals, however, it seems prudent for them to establish an independent foundation for the purpose. By passing corporate donations through to an independent foundation board, perhaps including community representatives, responsible to shareholders rather than to corporate management, the donor corporation's business goals, associated with profit-maximization, can be kept suitably distinct from philanthropic projects.

Nevertheless, despite their continuing interest, Carnegie's two ethical principles raise at least four general issues worthy of further discussion.

II. Current American Practice

If something like Carnegie's brand of philanthropy is essential to the flourishing of a liberal polity, then the attitudes and conduct of wealthy Americans are for the most part lamentable.[20] Available data suggest that although individuals are now giving more in total than ever, the wealthy pay little heed to Carnegie's second principle. For example, "top wealthholders tend to give away only a tiny percentage of wealth during their lifetimes," typically less than half of one percent of net wealth for the year prior to death.[21] They tend to wait until death to give: "In the aggregate, [their] charitable bequests represent over 20 times the amount of charitable contributions in a single year."[22]

Moreover, largely as a result of legislative changes in which the Tax Reform Act of 1969 figures prominently, fewer and fewer wealthy donors seem to be prepared to create private foundations to administer their holdings during their lifetimes. Instead, "since 1970 there has been a decrease in the formation of charitable corporations and an increase in the number of testamentary trusts."[23] Some evidence exists that tax attorneys are encouraging this pattern of large bequests and small lifetime gifts, as well as a shift away from private foundations to public charities, including community foundations.[24] And, unfortunately, the 1986 Tax Reform Act is likely to exacerbate matters by discouraging all forms of charity including volunteering.[25] The distinctive liberal kind of philanthropy associated with Carnegie's gospel is under siege, and is perhaps even in some danger of withering away.[26]

Despite the current situation, however, some wealthy Americans still cling to something like Carnegie's philanthropic manifesto. According to Teresa Odendahl's analysis of recent interviews with over 135 millionaires, some rich families continue actively to dispose of their surplus through private foundations and view conspicuous consumption with distaste. These people seem to support what Odendahl calls an "ideology," that is, the sort of liberal "middle way" referred to by Curti in which capitalism, philanthropy, and constitutional democracy all have key roles to play. Moreover, family tradition is apparently an important factor underlying attitudes and conduct, with some families exercising leadership in particular communities for generations. Nevertheless, these traditions may become increasingly difficult to preserve in a modern mass society.[27]

III. Liberal Justification of Carnegie's Gospel

A second general issue is whether the increasing abandonment in practice of Carnegie's gospel is a bad thing. The key concern here is to find a coherent liberal justification of the principles. Both

capitalists and constitutional democrats may be expected for different reasons to entertain serious doubts. For example, isn't the
first principle simply at odds with property rights? Don't the
wealthy have a right to pass on their property to their descendants?
Even if this conflict can be cleared up, isn't the second principle
at odds with democracy? Why does morality apparently prescribe
active giving by the wealthy themselves rather than simply government redistribution through progressive taxation? Shouldn't the rich
feel free to leave the administration of charity entirely to democratic
officials? Why is it wrong, as opposed to merely inefficient, for
government alone to oversee the provision of public goods? And
what should be done if the wealthy refuse even when encouraged
to give actively during their lifetimes? These sorts of questions must
be answered persuasively to justify philanthropy along the lines
proposed by Carnegie.

To examine how Carnegie himself seems to have answered them
is instructive. For convenience, my analysis is organized around
each of his two principles in turn.

The First Principle

According to the first principle, property owners are morally
obligated to give to the community some of the property to which
they are legally entitled. That seems to imply no great respect on
Carnegie's part for the law of private property. Yet he explicitly
defends the capitalist system, including its "intense Individualism"
and "great inequality," as the engine of "our wonderful material
development, which brings improved conditions in its train." In his
view, even if socialism is a "nobler ideal" in theory, "it is not
practicable in our day or in our age" because "it necessitates the
changing of human nature itself—a work of eons, even if it were
good to change it, which we cannot know."[28] Given human nature
as we know it, he suggests, some form of capitalism is best for the
foreseeable future. Most people simply will not work efficiently
unless they are assigned rights to the fruits of their own labor and
saving. Carnegie rejects any attempt to overturn the institution of
private property until human nature has evolved sufficiently to
realize "Swedenborg's idea of heaven, where . . . the angels derive
their happiness, not from laboring for self, but for each other."
Instead of indulging in such revolutionary folly, he says:

Our duty is with what is practicable now—with the next step possible in our own day and generation. . . . We might as well urge the destruction of the highest existing type of man because he failed to reach our ideal as to favor the destruction of Individualism, Private Property, the Law of Accumulation of Wealth, and the Law of Competition; for these are the highest result of human experience, the soil in which society, so far, has produced the best fruit.[29]

Despite his admiration for capitalism, however, Carnegie acknowledges that the existing economic arrangements are far from perfect: "often there is friction between the employer and the employed, between capital and labor, between rich and poor."[30] Indeed, he concedes that capitalism in its present form is perhaps even unjust. Although capitalism is "the best and most valuable" economic system "that humanity has yet accomplished" and remains "essential to the future progress of the race," the *present* laws and customs of private property are not beyond criticism and should be reformed if that would promote "the best interests" of the community.[31] This interpretation of Carnegie's philosophy of life is compatible with his well-known objections to contemporary property arrangements, in particular, the laws of inheritance. Moreover, it may help to clarify his *capitalist* rationale for urging the wealthy to distribute surplus wealth to which they and their families are entitled under the law. Society's legal definition of private property may be morally unattractive as it stands even if capitalism in some revised form should be defended.

To illustrate the point, a striking implication of Carnegie's first principle deserves emphasis: private property should be reformed to limit sharply any individual's right to inherit wealth. According to Carnegie, "surplus wealth . . . left to the families of the decedents . . . is the most injudicious" of the three possible modes of disposition he identifies (the other two modes are bequests and lifetime gifts for public purposes).[32] Indeed, "a great obstacle to the adoption of the gospel of wealth" is "the desire, futile as vain, to found or maintain hereditary families."[33] With rare exceptions, he claims, enormous legacies are inspired by "the vanity of the parents, rather than a wise regard for the good of the children." In his view, it is indisputable that a large legacy, and, by implication, a large lifetime gift to an individual, "generally deadens the talents and energies" of the recipient, to his own detriment as well as that of the community.[34] Harmful intergenerational transmission of surplus wealth ought to be discouraged, he thinks, by a graduated inheritance tax rising to a ceiling of "at least" fifty percent of the rich man's estate at his death.[35]

Carnegie's opposition to legacies beyond modest limits is so strong that it leads him into disagreement with William Gladstone. Gladstone favors the hereditary transmission of wealth and rank through entails of land and of businesses.[36] His view seems to be that wealth is made responsible if it is attached visibly to one's customary social station. He recalls that "when the principal form of property was the possession of land," for example, "wealth and station . . . were seen to be placed in proximity, at every point, with the discharge of duty; and as the neglect of this duty was in the public eye, they were in a partial yet real way responsible." But when property mainly consists of assets like capital equipment, stocks, and bonds, ownership becomes less visible and there is danger of "what may be called irresponsible wealth: wealth little watched and checked by opinion, little brought into immediate contact with duty."[37] To counteract that danger, he recommends that industrial enterprises as well as landholdings should be identified with particular families whose pride and ambition are thus visibly linked to public duty: "I rejoice to see it among our merchants, bankers, publishers: I wish it were commoner among our great manufacturing capitalists."[38]

So-called irresponsible wealth is not quite what Carnegie means by surplus wealth. Irresponsible wealth apparently includes real capital stock free of entails, for example, but capital goods are not surplus wealth. Indeed, Carnegie dismisses Gladstone's aristocratic vision of society as fatal to both economic efficiency and "republican simplicity." The managerial talents essential to a successful capitalist economy are not something that can be transmitted through a particular family: "The transmission of wealth and rank, without regard to merit or qualifications, may pass from one peer to another . . . without serious injury, since the duties are a matter of routine, seldom involving the welfare or means of others; but the management of business, never."[39] Moreover, the honor and civic virtue essential to a successful constitutional democracy are linked "almost without exception" to a "lineage of honest poverty—of laborious, wage-receiving parents, leading lives of virtuous pri-

vation, sacrificing comforts that their sons might be kept at school—
lineage from the cottage of poverty, not the palace of hereditary
rank and position."[40] In short, capitalism and democracy both work
well, he thinks, only if individuals willing to work have a more or
less equal opportunity to compete for managerial and political
posts. Hereditary transmission of wealth and rank is incompatible
with equal opportunity, and so with the "best interests" of the
community.

Like Gladstone, Carnegie believes that the good of the community
depends upon the high intellectual and moral capacities of its leading members. But unlike Gladstone, he argues that those high
capacities can be developed and maintained *only* through sustained
exercise.[41] For Carnegie, nobility is not the birthright of a hereditary
elite. Instead, noble capacities and dispositions must be acquired
through hard work and competition. This might almost be called
the axiom of liberal community. Moreover, it follows that enormous
bequests tend to harm recipients by encouraging sloth: "poverty
and struggle are advantageous" for improving character. Large gifts
to individuals further harm the community by tempting recipients
to hoard or conspicuously consume their surplus rather than investing it for the benefit of their fellows.[42]

The Second Principle

According to the second principle, the wealthy are morally obligated to distribute their surplus wealth during their lifetime in
ways that will actually benefit the community. But to do genuine
good and not mischief, Carnegie believes, wealthy people must
systematically study, with the help of experts, if necessary, the likely
consequences of alternative gifts, including the likely effects on the
recipients' characters. Serious complications are apparently caused
for philanthropists by the fact that whereas a gift per se may provide
immediate benefits, the consequences of relying on these gifts may
be of far more harm to able-bodied recipients. A calculating "scientific philanthropy" is essential to avoid "the evil produced by
indiscriminate giving."[43]

Indeed, Carnegie's view is that indiscriminate gifts are "one of
the serious obstacles to the improvement of our race."[44] He evidently
agrees with Josephine Shaw Lowell's statement that such giving

tends to impair the characters of its recipients: "Almsgiving and doleging [two forms of poor relief that do not discriminate between able-bodied and disabled recipients] are hurtful to those who receive them because they lead men to remit their own exertions and depend on others, upon whom they have no real claim, for the necessaries of life."[45] Indiscriminate giving is false charity based not on any rational expectation of beneficent consequences but rather on thoughtless benevolence, blind pity, or perhaps a selfish desire to avoid persistent requests: "[H]owever benevolent may be the motive, if the action be not beneficent, there is no charity. Almsgiving and doleging are hurtful—therefore they are not charitable."[46] By contrast, true charity is giving calculated to stimulate self-help and self-improvement: "There is really no true charity except that which will help others to help themselves, and place within the reach of the aspiring the means to climb."[47] To be truly philanthropic, the wealthy have a duty to the community *not* to give indiscriminately:

> Neither the individual nor the race is improved by almsgiving. . . .
> [T]he only true reformer . . . is as careful and as anxious not to aid the unworthy, and, perhaps, even more so, for in almsgiving more injury is probably done by rewarding vice than by relieving virtue.[48]

The discrimination required for true charity appears to have been an important factor underlying Carnegie's rejection of bequests for public purposes as a desirable mode of distributing surplus wealth: "The cases are not few in which the real object sought by the testator is not attained. . . . It is well to remember that it requires the exercise of not less ability than that which acquires it, to use wealth so as to be really beneficial to the community."[49] In short, the wealthy have a duty to make sure, as far as possible, that their surplus wealth is not used indiscriminately. At the same time, of course, testators who leave vast sums to be administered by others "may fairly be thought men who would not have left it at all had they been able to take it with them."[50]

Carnegie's gospel, then, recommends lifetime gifts carefully designed permanently to uplift the community by promoting the self-improvement of its members: "[T]he millionaire [should] take care that the purposes for which he [gives his surplus wealth] . . . shall not have a degrading, pauperizing, tendency upon its recipients, but that his trust shall be so administered as to stimulate the best and most aspiring poor of the community to further efforts for their own improvement."[51] "What we must seek . . . for surplus wealth, if we are to work genuine good, are uses which give nothing for nothing, which require cooperation, self-help, and which, by no possibility, can tend to sap the spirit of manly independence, which is the only sure foundation upon which the steady improvement of our race can be built."[52] The best uses of wealth, he makes clear, are gifts to build universities, free libraries, hospitals, scientific laboratories, museums, halls, parks, and the like. Those gifts provide opportunities for people to improve themselves "in body and mind."[53] Conspicuously absent are gifts of cash or goods in kind to the needy poor.

Yet Carnegie certainly does not deny society's obligation to guarantee the necessities of life to all: "Common humanity impels us . . . to see, through our poor laws, that none die of starvation, and to provide comfortable shelter, clothing, and instruction."[54] Moreover, "our assistance . . . should *never* be withheld in times of accident, illness, or other exceptional cause."[55] His point is that each person should have a legal right to those things, conditional, where possible, "upon work performed." The policy of "indoor relief" that both he and Lowell favor seems harsh by contemporary standards. But that government has a duty to enact suitable laws guaranteeing to all some basic standard of subsistence is not questioned.[56] By implication, general taxpayers—not wealthy philanthropists—have the responsibility to provide necessities like poor relief.[57]

The implied division of responsibilities between government and philanthropy correlates nicely to the familiar natural law distinction between justice and charity, whereby citizens are held to have equal moral rights in matters of justice but no moral rights in matters of charity. Carnegie and Lowell, like many of their contemporaries, apparently take that classical distinction for granted, with the implication that liberal philanthropy must not be expected to do the work of a just government. In their view, provision of poor relief by the wealthy should only be contemplated in the event of government's failure to respect the equal rights of citizens to basic subsistence. Government failure warrants strong protest, of course, and liberal philanthropists have both a moral obligation and an incentive to lead the protest. Even if this explains why a wealthy philanthropist like Carnegie is reluctant to engage in public relief, however, it does not tell us why government itself should refrain from taking over true philanthropy by suitably taxing away Carnegie's surplus. After all, the gospel of wealth admits that the rich are merely administrators of that wealth on behalf of the community. Why not rely exclusively on public administrators more or less subject to popular control?

One answer comes from Lowell: charity is defined as voluntary giving, in which case "all official and public relief is . . . outside the pale of charity, since it lacks the voluntary element."[58] But to that answer a radical democrat may well reply: do away with charity altogether as you define it, then, and legally force the taxpayer to finance all the universities, museums, parks, and the like that elected representatives decide are justified. Without further argument, a fair reply is that political leaders alone should be responsible for promoting the good of the community.

A more substantial answer is pluralist, that wealthy philanthropists should be permitted to compete with government to provide a greater variety of public goods than might otherwise be the case. As J. S. Mill puts it: "The truth needs reasserting, and needs it every day more and more, that what the improvement of mankind and of all of their works most imperatively demands is variety, not uniformity."[59] But even to that answer the radical democrat may fairly respond: anything philanthropy can do, government can and perhaps should do too. In other words, government's role in the provision of public goods is unlimited in principle, even if wealthy philanthropists should also be granted a subsidiary role. By implication, nothing is distinctive about philanthropy, and its proper scope is entirely at the discretion of political leaders.

But Carnegie apparently relies largely on a third answer that also seems to be decisive for his contemporaries like Lowell and Mill: A liberal government cannot discriminate justifiably among worthy and unworthy recipients as required for true charity. The problem is *not* that government officials are necessarily less competent or more corrupt than wealthy philanthropists or foundation administrators. Indeed, we have little reason to expect either government officials or private philanthropists to be paragons of virtue in the absence of suitable legal checks on their conduct. Rather, the problem is that liberal justice requires government to "act by general rule," that is, according to laws and policies that do not discriminate between citizens merely on the basis of their character. By contrast, liberal philanthropy requires discrimination precisely on that basis, and is not extended to able-bodied individuals or communities known to be unwilling to help themselves. In short, the *means* essential to liberal justice are incompatible with those intrinsic to liberal philanthropy. Just political leaders will tend to do more real harm than good through indiscriminate giving if they attempt to usurp the role of independent philanthropists. As Mill summarizes: "The state . . . cannot undertake to discriminate between the deserving and the undeserving indigent. . . . Private charity can make these distinctions."[60]

In this light, government and philanthropy have distinct purposes. If government tries to discriminate as true charity requires, then it acts unjustly, contrary to the rule of law. But if government gives indiscriminately all sorts of public goods, then it simply encourages degrading dependence on the state, the very reverse of beneficence, because working taxpayers may choose to become idle without losing the goods. This policy tends to hinder, in other words, the possibility of liberal community.[61] It follows that a liberal government is justly limited to the provision of only those public goods that all citizens, and all communities, within its jurisdiction may reasonably be said to need. Liberal philanthropy, on the other hand, is properly a distinct activity whose chief purpose is to provide what are considered luxury public goods that permit citizens to explore tastes beyond their customary needs. At any given point in time, a wealthy philanthropist or private foundation may properly give one community but not another a free library, for example, if working members of the first but not the second show they are serious about self-improvement by agreeing to contribute matching funds, through user fees or local taxes, for operating and maintenance costs.[62] But a liberal government cannot properly provide public goods to one community and then turn around and deny that those same goods are needed elsewhere. If tax dollars are used to build a free library for one community, then government must acknowledge that every community in its jurisdiction has an equal claim, even if some will not agree to maintain and support their libraries. The latter may well press their claims to get something for nothing, construction jobs are jobs after all. Yet deteriorating buildings with meager collections that pass for "libraries" are unlikely to do much good.

Notice that philanthropy itself may cause the government-philanthropic division of functions to evolve in practice, by altering social customs. What was once thought a luxury may come to be considered a need, if large numbers acquire a taste for it. If most acquire a taste for reading or for advanced studies so that it becomes customary to consider possession of the abilities in question a necessity, then philanthropy may safely share their cultivation with government. In that case, most every taxpayer under the government's jurisdiction now considers libraries and universities necessary for all, and will fully pay for his own use of those goods. Such taxpayers are simply workers of high moral and intellectual capacity who agree to help themselves by way of government. Moreover, that changing partnership between government and philanthropy need not in principle ever involve indiscriminate giving. Indeed, gifts to those who will not help themselves, whether provided by government, by individual citizens, or by private corporations (non-profit or for-profit), tend to destroy the community by encouraging the dependence with which we seem to be increasingly familiar.

Even if we accept all this, however, the question remains: what should be done if the wealthy simply refuse to give during their lifetimes? Carnegie does mention estate tax rates of at least fifty percent to discourage the "vain and futile desire" to establish a dynasty. But his main emphasis seems to be on a suitable evolution of the opinions and customs of the wealthy themselves: the rich who care about their reputations, he thinks, will increasingly adopt the gospel of wealth to avoid dying "disgraced."[63] That this sort of development has not occurred is pretty clear. Instead, the ethos of Veblen's leisure class seem to have been democratized. Before taking up this important question, however, I want to comment briefly on possible sources of Carnegie's liberal ethic of philanthropy.

IV. Continuity with British Liberal Values

A third general issue concerns possible intellectual sources of Carnegie's thinking. One important source is, of course, the gospel of Christ, with the caveat that Carnegie's own religious faith is not restricted to any official creed.[64] A second important source is American Individualism, particularly the writings of Emerson. Indeed, Carnegie may have deliberately cast his gospel as a solution to what Emerson sees as "the problem of civilization," that is, "how to give all access to the masterpieces of art and nature."[65] But the source I wish to underscore is classical British liberalism, epitomized for Carnegie by the works of Herbert Spencer and J. S. Mill. Gladstone himself points to the influence of liberalism on Carnegie's character: "There is no hardier liberalism in this island than that which has flourished in Dundee."[66]

Carnegie openly acknowledges that the works of Spencer and Darwin "were revelations to me . . . ; what the law of gravitation did for matter, the law of evolution did for mind."[67] But that should not be taken to imply his acceptance in detail of Spencer's political economy. For example, Spencer adamantly defends complete freedom of bequest as essential to human evolution, contrary to Carnegie's philosophy of life.[68] Recall that Carnegie also has the highest praise for Gladstone, despite his defense of inheritance.

Carnegie also praises Mill's works, and even acknowledges himself to be a "thorough disciple" on the tariff question.[69] But how closely the gospel of wealth mirrors Mill's own ideas is not sufficiently appreciated. A brief comparison is in order.[70] Like Carnegie, Mill rejects socialist revolution in favor of gradual reform of the capitalist system for the foreseeable future.[71] He also argues that unlimited inheritance is no part of capitalism at its best, primarily because recipients do not deserve to get money for which they have not worked or saved.[72] He implies as well that capitalists have no moral right to excess profits, but instead are properly viewed as trustees of that wealth on behalf of the community.[73] And he claims that citizens have equal basic rights to at most some customary level of living; that government has a duty to provide that basic minimum to all; and that individual philanthropists can and should give in ways that promote self-help, recognizing that indiscriminate giving tends to degrade recipients by encouraging habits of dependence.[74]

Clearly, the gist of Carnegie's message is already present in the writings of Mill, probably the most influential liberal thinker of the century. My intention is not to depreciate Carnegie's originality,

An Ideal Liberal Polity

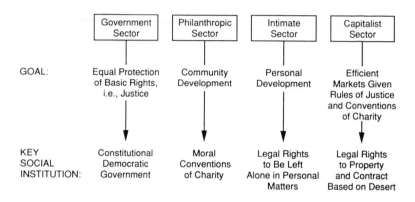

	Government Sector	Philanthropic Sector	Intimate Sector	Capitalist Sector
GOAL:	Equal Protection of Basic Rights, i.e., Justice	Community Development	Personal Development	Efficient Markets Given Rules of Justice and Conventions of Charity
KEY SOCIAL INSTITUTION:	Constitutional Democratic Government	Moral Conventions of Charity	Legal Rights to Be Left Alone in Personal Matters	Legal Rights to Property and Contract Based on Desert

however, but to emphasize that his philanthropic manifesto is best understood in terms of liberal values. By implication, American philanthropy represents at least in part the flowering of an Anglo-American liberal tradition.

The Carnegie-Mill perspective encourages us to keep in mind an ideal liberal polity or "middle way" in which capitalism, philanthropy, and limited democratic government coexist in harmony. Carnegie, for example, asks us to imagine "a reign of harmony, another ideal, differing, indeed, from that of the Communist in requiring only the further evolution of existing conditions, not the overthrow of our civilization."[75] And, as I have argued at length elsewhere, Mill similarly envisions an ideal liberal polity as the goal of reform.[76] The figure suggests the main spheres or sectors of that ideal polity, where the sectors involve distinct purposes even though the institutions must be interrelated in various ways. It avoids the troublesome terms public and private because of their various connotations.[77]

Carnegie for most of his life seems more optimistic than Mill about attaining some such liberal democratic ideal. "This day already dawns" is not a statement we could expect to find in the latter's writings, given his fears that a despotism of ignorant mass opinion and custom would lead to stagnation and decline in

Britain.[78] Of course, Carnegie's greater optimism was itself shattered by World War I. But before the war, he seems to have insisted upon a peculiar Spencerian brand of evolutionism. He apparently had faith that human evolution manifests the will of a Supreme Creator whose name "matters not." Evolution is the Creator's way of unfolding the perfection of mankind.[79] That sort of a priori belief is precisely what Mill could never accept about Spencer's philosophy, even though both he and Spencer agreed that this epistemological divergence was greatly outweighed by their practical agreement on liberal doctrine.[80]

V. Conclusion: Liberal Possibilities

A final issue is the feasibility of reinvigorating the American philanthropic tradition symbolized by Carnegie's gospel. What should be done to foster and preserve the liberal spirit of philanthropy that I think is essential to America's "middle way"? How might *liberal* moral conventions about charity be developed to promote an ideal liberal polity? Certain legal reforms are important for this purpose. But even more important is public education, including learning by doing good for the community, under the leadership of the churches and the school system, in particular, universities. Indeed, unless appropriate dispositions are inculcated in young people, popular support for the requisite legal reforms cannot reasonably be expected. Any liberal polity relies in part on virtuous traits in its citizenry, including a disposition to help others conjoined with intelligence to discern the probable consequences of one's conduct.[81]

Carnegie's gospel of wealth suggests various legal changes that should be considered seriously by Americans seeking to foster an atmosphere in which liberal habits of philanthropy and community service might breathe.[82] Ironically, given the Carnegie-Mill penchant for gradual social change, the legal reforms in question have now almost a radical air about them. In any case, reforms such as the following are essential for promoting a liberal American polity:

—sharply progressive federal taxation of all gifts and bequests to able-bodied individuals beyond some moderate ceiling (for example, the cost of a higher education and / or of an average home), so that large holdings of surplus wealth will tend to be dispersed among many recipients to avoid taxation (such dispersion is not really encouraged under the current policies involving a maximum fifty percent tax rate on gifts and estates valued at $2.5 million and over with special exemptions for trusts);

—sharply progressive taxation of luxury expenditures, to discourage ostentatious living;

—equal tax treatment for private foundations and public charities, as opposed to the current bias established by the 1969 Tax Reform Act against the former;

—a requirement that for-profit corporations should establish independent "pass-through" foundations (that is, legal entities under independent management) for any disbursement of corporate profits for philanthropic purposes; the establishment, management and specific disbursements of the independent foundation should be subject to approval by a majority of the donor corporation's shareholders at an open public meeting (so that shareholders' democracy would be exposed to local community views when funding philanthropic projects in that community);

—unlimited charitable deductions from taxable income for itemizers, including shareholders of for-profit corporations who agree to disburse their dividends through an independent foundation for community purposes; as well as restoration of a minimum charitable deduction for non-itemizers;

—a substantial increase (say, doubling) of the required annual payout rate (currently five percent of investment assets) for private foundations, as a means of underscoring the goal of philanthropy as opposed to perpetual growth of foundation assets;

—perhaps even a constitutional amendment to permit suitable public recognition of extraordinary philanthropy during one's lifetime, for example, a ceremonial Order of Benefactors of the U.S. with terms and conditions of membership to be fixed in Article 1, section 9, no formal political privileges attaching to membership.

These kinds of reforms would go a long way toward reviving liberal philanthropy in America, although we cannot be optimistic about the prospects for their implementation. Even if implemented, they would not force any individual to give for philanthropic purposes during his lifetime. Still, suitable laws can strongly discourage adverse attitudes such as exclusive love of family and taste for ostentation. People who persist in acting on the basis of these attitudes will have to pay dearly through the tax system, thereby reducing, at least in principle, the general tax burden for the rest of us.

Nevertheless, a package of legal changes, however perfectly designed, cannot by itself engender liberal philanthropy and community. Clearly, laws alone cannot generate the disposition to help others or the intellectual discrimination required for liberal moral virtue. Only a suitable liberal education can hope to do this. Church and school officials must take the lead in evoking in young people a liberal character, including a disposition to help the community and an intellectual capacity to assess the likely outcomes of various types of aid. Universities could facilitate this by undertaking curriculum reforms that engage more faculty and students in community service, including volunteer work for local libraries, museums, and environmental groups as well as for various organizations designed to support disadvantaged minorities. After all is said and done, of course, some individuals might still never be motivated by anything stronger than their own immediate material interest. Perhaps there will always be what Gladstone calls "that class of men, amongst all the most miserable, for whom the word 'surplus' can never exist."[83] But liberalism is characteristically optimistic that men and women are capable of much better, that the class of misers can be rendered insignificant by suitable laws and moral conventions. A passion to hoard is neither so innate nor sufficiently strong in many people that it can withstand public contempt of an educated community.[84]

Moral and political advocacy is required to prevent further decline of philanthropic activity, the one feature of modern American life that is both individualistic and communitarian. That tradition of giving is crucial to the flourishing of both the individual and the community, and is deservedly cherished. After all, as Mill so eloquently says: "Among the works of man, which human life is rightly employed in perfecting and beautifying, the first in importance surely is man himself."[85] Isn't that what the love of man is really all about?

Notes

1. "From Charity to Philanthropy" [1962], in Daniel Boorstin, *Hidden History* (New York: Harper & Row, 1987), pp. 205–206. Unlike Boorstin, I do not distinguish between the terms charity and philanthropy for present purposes. According to what I am calling the liberal view, either term means beneficence or doing good for other people, and excludes unwise gifts that (although inspired by love or pity) actually do net harm. Thus, liberal philanthropy is restricted to beneficence whatever the agent's motivation; whereas non-liberal philanthropy affirms benevolence as both necessary and sufficient for doing good, whatever the consequences.

2. Merle Curti, "American Philanthropy and the National Character," *American Quarterly* 10 (1958): 436.

3. See also Michael Novak, *The Spirit of Democratic Capitalism* (New York: Simon & Schuster/American Enterprise Institute, 1982), esp. pp. 143–155, 333–360. He speaks of "the communitarian individual" who understands that "the highest good of the political economy of democratic capitalism is to be suffused by *caritas*" (p. 357; emphasis in original). Such an individual is, in other words, able to recognize that "the love of friends for one another is . . . the way by which humans *participate* in the life of God"; and motivated to guide his conduct accordingly (p. 355; emphasis in original). On one interpretation, Novak is painting a religious gloss on an ideal liberal polity: "Caritas is at one and the same time an ideal of individual autonomy . . . and an ideal of community" (p. 358).

4. For an introduction to the modern debate, see Robert Payton, *Major Challenges to Philanthropy* (Washington, D.C.: Independent Sector, 1984); and Virginia A. Hodgkinson et al., *The Future of the Nonprofit Sector: Challenges, Changes and Policy Considerations* (San Francisco: Jossey-Bass, 1989).

5. See, for example, Barry Karl, "Philanthropy, Policy Planning, and the Bureaucratization of the Democratic Ideal," *Daedalus* 105 (Fall 1976): 129–149; Barry Karl and Stanley Katz, "The American Private Philanthropic Foundation and the Public Sphere 1890–1930," *Minerva* 19 (1981): 236–270; and Barry Karl and Stanley Katz, "Foundations and Ruling Class Elites," *Daedalus* 116 (Winter 1987): 1–40.

6. Lester Salamon calls for a new theory of government-nonprofit partnership in his "Partners in Public Service: The Scope and Theory of Government-Nonprofit Relations," in W. Powell, ed., *The Nonprofit Sector: A Research Handbook* (New Haven and London: Yale University Press, 1987), pp. 99–117. See also Jon Van Til, *Mapping the Third Sector: Voluntarism in a Changing Social Economy* (New York: The Foundation Center, 1988); and Hodgkinson et al., *Future of the Nonprofit Sector.*

7. In Weber's famous view, originally published in 1904–5, the capitalist disposition to accumulate wealth yet forgo ostentatious consumption has its roots in the Protestant duty to succeed in a worldly "calling" to promote the glory of god. Under Calvinism, fulfilment of that duty became a sign of one's election by god to salvation. In short, the Calvinist must have

faith in his election; and must carefully calculate how to do good in this world as a sign of his faith. As W. K. Jordan explains: "The Protestant clergy, being Calvinist, could not argue that good works were necessary to grace, but they did hold with a most persuasive and sustained vehemence that good works were an authentic and a necessary fruit of grace categorically demanded of His saints by God. . . . The Calvinist not only said but he believed that we are but stewards of wealth for which we are accountable to God" (p. 152). Thus, capitalist entrepreneurship and liberal philanthropy emerge rather paradoxically from blind obedience to religious authority. For insights into the modern evolution of Anglo-American philanthropy, see W. K. Jordan, *Philanthropy in England, 1480–1660* (London: Allen & Unwin, 1959); and David Owen, *English Philanthropy, 1660–1960* (Cambridge, Mass.: Harvard University Press, 1964). For Weber's argument, see Max Weber, *The Protestant Ethic and the Spirit of Capitalism,* 2d ed., trans. Talcott Parsons (London: Allen & Unwin, 1976). Although he does not necessarily accept Weber's perspective, Thomas Haskell has recently argued that the rise of capitalism during the period 1750–1850 is associated with an expansion of the individual's causal horizon, and that this heightened sense of agency brought with it a new "humanitarian sensibility" and awareness of one's moral responsibilities. By implication, moral conventions (including those of philanthropy) have altered significantly under capitalism. See Haskell, "Capitalism and the Origins of the Humanitarian Sensibility, Parts I & II," *American Historical Review* 90 (1985): 339–361, 547–566; and subsequent Forum involving Haskell, David Brion Davis, and John Ashworth, *American Historical Review* 92 (1987): 797–878.

8. "Poor Richard's Almanac Improved, 1748," in *Benjamin Franklin: Writings,* ed. J. A. Leo Lemay (New York: The Library of America, 1987), p. 1247.

9. It should be emphasized that the distinction between liberal and non-liberal philanthropy does not correspond to the distinction between Christian (or, more generally, religious) and secular charity. The first distinction is essentially one between calculated beneficence and blind pity or benevolence. The second distinction hinges on the agent's motivation for doing good. A Calvinist may carefully calculate how she can best help her community, for example, because she is motivated to find signs of her own election and to promote god's glory in this world. Thus, she practices liberal philanthropy for religious reasons. Or, to take another example, a pagan may thoughtlessly divert his wealth to wasteful community projects because he habitually conforms to prevailing majority opinion in that community. Thus, he practices non-liberal philanthropy for purely secular reasons.

10. "The Gospel of Wealth" [1889], in E. C. Kirkland, ed., *The Gospel of Wealth and Other Timely Essays* (Cambridge: Harvard University Press, 1962), pp. 14–49. Also reprinted in this volume.

11. As Robert Heilbroner remarks: "[I]t is not enough to conclude that Carnegie was in fact a smaller man than he conceived himself. For this

judgment overlooks one immense and irrefutable fact. He did, in the end, abide by his self-imposed duty. He did give nearly all of his gigantic fortune away. . . . Carnegie is something of America writ large. . . . In his curious triumph, we see what we hope is our own steadfast core of integrity." Robert Heilbroner, "Carnegie and Rockefeller," in Byron Dobell, ed., *A Sense of History: The Best Writing from the Pages of American Heritage* (Boston: Houghton Mifflin, 1985), pp. 442–443. On the more general point, see also Barry Karl, "The Moral Basis of Capitalist Philanthropy," in *Spring Research Forum Working Papers: Philanthropy, Voluntary Action, and the Public Good* (Washington, D.C.: Independent Sector, 1986), pp. 103–118; and Robert Nisbet, "America as Utopia," *Reason* 18 (March 1987): 35–40.

12. Carnegie, "The Advantages of Poverty" [1891], in Kirkland, ed., *Gospel of Wealth*, p. 55.

13. "Gospel of Wealth," ibid., p. 25.

14. Ibid., p. 26.

15. "Advantages of Poverty," ibid., p. 72.

16. "Gospel of Wealth," ibid., p. 18.

17. Public goods are goods like free libraries, public parks, or even limited-access research laboratories that cannot be efficiently provided through the market because users who refuse to pay a full price (so-called "free riders") cannot or should not be excluded from using the goods once produced. Government may thus decide to legally coerce everyone to finance the goods through taxes. Alternatively, individuals or groups may decide to voluntarily pay a disproportionate part (perhaps all) of the costs of the goods, because of motivations other than immediate material self-interest, for example, benevolence.

18. "Gospel of Wealth," ibid., p. 48.

19. See Carnegie, *Autobiography* [1920], ed. J. Van Dyke (Boston: Northeastern University Press, 1986).

20. I do not mean to imply that charitable attitudes and conduct of the wealthy may have been any better in the past.

21. Eugene Steuerle, "Charitable Giving Patterns of the Wealthy," in Teresa Odendahl, ed., *America's Wealthy and the Future of Foundations* (New York: Foundation Center, 1987), p. 207. The results are based on a sample of matched estate and income tax returns filed during the mid-1970s. Steuerle indicates that annual gifts do not appear to be unusual for the year prior to death.

22. Ibid.

23. Elizabeth Boris, "Creation and Growth: A Survey of Private Foundations," ibid., p. 73. Not only are the numbers of new foundations declining, so is the relative financial importance of foundations in the economy. See Ralph Nelson, "An Economic History of Large Foundations," ibid., pp. 127–177.

24. Francis Ostrower, "The Role of Advisors to the Wealthy," ibid., pp. 247–265.

25. For some preliminary evidence, see Charles T. Clotfelter, *The Impact*

of Tax Reform on Charitable Giving: a 1989 Perspective. Working Paper 26 (Durham: Duke University Center for the Study of Philanthropy and Volunteering, 1990).

26. See Brian O'Connell, "Private Philanthropy and the Preservation of a Free and Democratic Society," in Robert Payton et al., *Philanthropy: Four Views* (New Brunswick: Transaction Books, 1988), pp. 27–38.

27. Odendahl, "Wealthy Donors and Their Charitable Attitudes," in Odendahl, ed., *America's Wealthy*, pp. 223–246. Odendahl herself has recently criticized what she views as the elitist ideology associated with private philanthropy in the United States. She apparently rejects the appeal of what I am calling the liberal approach, and favors instead a more democratic philanthropy in which minority groups (including the poor) have more control over the sorts of projects funded by wealthy philanthropists. Rather than "uplift the community" by funding elitist institutions such as universities and museums, philanthropy should concentrate on poor relief and on supporting the activities of disadvantaged minorities. Although her call for a redirection of private giving is understandable in light of the shameful recent cuts in federal social programs, Odendahl simply ignores the classical liberal perspective on philanthropy and takes for granted that minority groups have a moral right to use other people's wealth for purposes rejected by the latter. See Teresa Odendahl, *Charity Begins at Home: Generosity and Self-Interest Among the Philanthropic Elite* (New York: Basic Books, 1990).

28. "Gospel of Wealth," in Kirkland, ed., *Gospel of Wealth*, pp. 14–19.

29. Ibid., pp. 18–19. See also "Advantages of Poverty," ibid., pp. 75–76.

30. "Gospel of Wealth," ibid., p. 16.

31. Ibid., p. 19.

32. Ibid., pp. 19–20.

33. "Advantages of Poverty," ibid., p. 59.

34. Ibid., p. 56.

35. "Gospel of Wealth," ibid., p. 22. At the same time, Carnegie remarks that "it is difficult to set bounds to the share of a rich man's estate which should go at his death to the public through the agency of the State."

36. "Mr. Carnegie's 'Gospel of Wealth': A Review and a Recommendation" [1890], in B. J. Hendrick, ed., *Miscellaneous Writings of Andrew Carnegie* (Garden City, N.Y.: Doubleday, Doran & Co., 1933), vol. 2, pp. 136–139.

37. Ibid., p. 129.

38. Ibid., p. 138.

39. "Advantages of Poverty," in Kirkland, ed., *Gospel of Wealth*, pp. 57–58.

40. Ibid., pp. 62–63.

41. It should be noted that, inheritance aside, Gladstone is essentially in sympathy with Carnegie's gospel. Relying on his memory of what he calls the "Universal Beneficent Society," he suggests that the wealthy should

form a voluntary beneficent association, binding themselves in honor to donate some fixed annual proportion of their incomes ("fixed, that is to say, by themselves)" for philanthropic purposes. See "Mr. Carnegie's 'Gospel of Wealth,'" Hendrick, ed., *Miscellaneous Writings*, pp. 149–156. Reverend Hughes corrects Gladstone's faulty recollection of the British and Foreign Systematic Beneficence Society, a Christian association established in 1860 "to promote the principle and practice amongst all professing Christians" of giving away at least one-tenth of one's weekly income "for God and the poor." See "Irresponsible Wealth III," ibid., pp. 198–202. The tithe is salient, of course, in both Christian and Jewish religious traditions.

42. It is worth emphasizing that Carnegie sees the growth of a so-called leisure class as incompatible with American capitalism and democracy. As described by Thorstein Veblen and depicted in the novels of Henry James and Edith Wharton, the leisure class is an idle elite whose conspicuous consumption is supported largely by inherited wealth and motivated for the most part by a concern to emulate European aristocracy.

43. "Advantages of Poverty," in Kirkland, ed., *Gospel of Wealth*, p. 69. See also John D. Rockefeller, "The Difficult Art of Giving" [1908–09], in *Random Reminiscences of Men and Events* (Tarrytown, N.Y.: Sleepy Hollow Press & Rockefeller Archive Center, 1984), pp. 90–106.

44. "Gospel of Wealth," in Kirkland, ed., *Gospel of Wealth*, p. 26.

45. Josephine Shaw Lowell, *Public Relief and Private Charity* [1884] (New York: Arno Press, 1971), p. 90. In the preface, Lowell describes her work as a "restatement of the principles upon which the modern methods of charity are based."

46. Ibid., p. 89.

47. Carnegie, "Advantages of Poverty," in Kirkland, ed., *Gospel of Wealth*, p. 68.

48. "Gospel of Wealth," ibid., p. 27. See also pp. 31–32; "Advantages of Poverty," pp. 67–69; and, more generally, Edward N. Saveth, "Patrician Philanthropy in America: The Late Nineteenth and Early Twentieth Centuries," *Social Service Review* 54 (1980): 76–91.

49. "Gospel of Wealth," in Kirkland, ed., *Gospel of Wealth*, p. 21.

50. Ibid.

51. Ibid., p. 31.

52. Carnegie, "The Best Uses of Wealth" [1895], in Hendrick, ed., *Miscellaneous Writings*, p. 210.

53. "Gospel of Wealth," in Kirkland, ed., *Gospel of Wealth*, p. 28.

54. "Advantages of Poverty," ibid., p. 68.

55. "Best Uses," in Hendrick, ed., *Miscellaneous Writings*, p. 208.

56. According to the "indoor relief" policy, poor relief to able-bodied people unwilling to help themselves should be administered "indoors," that is, in state workhouses where the "unfortunates" should be made to do some form of work for their basic subsistence. Those in the workhouse would thus be separated from the rest of society and should forfeit various rights enjoyed by other citizens, including the franchise and the right to

procreate. Disabled people would not be subject to this sort of stigma, of course, because they are by definition unable as opposed to unwilling to work. They should be supported by both government and philanthropy outside the workhouse. For an interesting argument that ambiguities in the term "disabled" opened the door to expansion of the welfare state, see Deborah Stone, *The Disabled State* (Philadelphia: Temple University Press, 1985).

57. Bernard Shaw also insists on this point in his inimitable style. See "Socialism for Millionaires," *Contemporary Review* 69 (1896): 204–217.

58. Lowell, *Public Relief,* p. 89.

59. "Endowments" [1869], in John Stuart Mill, *Collected Works,* J. M. Robson, gen. ed. (Toronto and London: University of Toronto Press and Routledge & Kegan Paul, 1965—), vol. 5, p. 617. See also "On Liberty" [1859], ibid., vol. 18, pp. 260–275.

60. *Principles of Political Economy* [1848], in Mill, *Collected Works,* vol. 3, p. 962.

61. For further development of the general theme, see Michael Taylor, *Community, Anarchy and Liberty* (Cambridge: Cambridge University Press, 1982).

62. Such was Carnegie's practice. See "The Gospel of Wealth," in Kirkland, ed., *Gospel of Wealth,* pp. 36–40.

63. Ibid., pp. 28–30.

64. Carnegie, "A Confession of Religious Faith," in Hendrick, ed., *Miscellaneous Writings,* pp. 291–319. On the religious tradition of philanthropy in America, see also Virginia Bernhard, "Cotton Mather and the Doing of Good: A Puritan Gospel of Wealth," *New England Quarterly* 49 (1976): 225–241.

65. R. W. Emerson, *The Conduct of Life* [1860], chapter III ("Wealth"), in *Emerson: Essays and Lectures,* J. Porte, ed. (New York: Library of America, 1983), p. 995. Emerson continues: "They should own who can administer; not they who hoard and conceal . . . but they whose work carves out work for more, opens a path for all. . . For he is the rich man in whom the people are rich." See also Emerson, "Gifts" [1844], ibid., pp. 535–538.

66. "Mr. Carnegie's 'Gospel of Wealth,'" Hendrick, ed., *Miscellaneous Writings,* p. 127. Carnegie was born in Dunfermline, "a radical town" in the vicinity of Dundee, Scotland.

67. Carnegie, "Confession of Religious Faith," ibid., p. 297.

68. Herbert Spencer, *The Principles of Ethics* [1897], ed. Tibor R. Machan (Indianapolis: Liberty Classics, 1978), vol 2., pp. 135–142. As Edward Kirkland suggests, Carnegie may have had a pretty casual understanding of Spencer's Law of Evolution. See Kirkland, ed., *Gospel of Wealth,* p. 81, n.2.

69. Carnegie, "Imperial Federation" [1891], in Kirkland, ed., *Gospel of Wealth,* pp. 216–217.

70. For a more complete discussion of Mill's view of capitalism, see my "Justice Under Capitalism," in J. Chapman and J. R. Pennock, eds.,

Markets and Justice: Nomos 31 (New York: New York University Press, 1989), pp. 122–162.

71. *Principles of Political Economy,* in Mill, *Collected Works,* vol. 3, pp. 765–796; and "Chapters on Socialism," ibid., vol. 5, pp. 727–753.

72. *Principles of Political Economy,* ibid., vol. 2, pp. 218–226.

73. Ibid., pp. 207–208, 215–217, 226–232.

74. Ibid., vol. 3, pp. 960–962, 968–970; and "Endowments," ibid., vol. 5, pp. 613–629.

75. "Gospel of Wealth," in Kirkland, ed., *Gospel of Wealth,* p. 23. See also p. 28.

76. See J. Riley, *Liberal Utilitarianism* (Cambridge: Cambridge University Press, 1988).

77. See, for example, Michael Novak, "An Essay on 'Public' and 'Private,'" in Payton et al., *Philanthropy,* pp. 11–25. I have discussed the public-private distinction at length elsewhere. See J. Riley, "Rights to Liberty in Purely Private Matters, Parts I & II," *Economics and Philosophy* 5 & 6 (1989/1990): 121–166, 27–64.

78. On this aspect of Mill's thought (reminiscent in many ways of earlier Country Whig pessimism), see J. W. Burrow, *Whigs and Liberals: Continuity and Change in English Political Thought* (Oxford: Clarendon Press, 1988), pp. 77–124.

79. Carnegie, "Confession of Religious Faith," in Hendrick, ed., *Miscellaneous Writings.* In some respects, Michael Novak's views are now reminiscent of this Spencer-Carnegie metaphysical perspective. See Novak, *The Spirit of Democratic Capitalism.*

80. Whereas Spencer supposes the individual is endowed genetically with some basic perceptions and norms that reflect the accumulated experience of the race, Mill suggests the individual has no such innate practical knowledge. Rather, for Mill, practical knowledge can be acquired by any person only after her mental capacities are called into action by her *own* experience of the actual world. Spencer's view implies that some basic moral concepts are known intuitively to us prior to our experience: we simply cannot conceive at least some things other than as we do because of those a priori ideas. Moreover, if evolution is taken to mean progress ordained by some superhuman Creator, then our inherited ideas and beliefs will necessarily improve as evolution proceeds. Mill denies all this. Even so, he and Spencer arrive at a large number of the same practical conclusions anyway, hence their general sympathy for one another's work. For the relevant debate between them, see, for example, J. S. Mill, *System of Logic* [1843], in *Collected Works,* vol. 7, pp. 262–279; Mill, *An Examination of Hamilton's Philosophy* [1865], in ibid., vol. 9, pp. 143–145; Mill's letter to Spencer of August 12, 1865, reprinted in ibid., vol. 16, pp. 1089–1091; Herbert Spencer, "Mill Versus Hamilton—The Test of Truth" [1865], in *Essays: Moral, Political and Aesthetic* (New York: Appleton, 1883), pp. 383–413; and Spencer, "Replies to Criticisms" [1881], in *Principles of Ethics,* vol. 2, pp. 483–504.

81. Evidently a liberal commitment to the rule of law does not imply

toleration for uncharitable ways of life nor indifference towards unkind traits of character. The rule of law implies only that rules should be impartial or neutral in the sense of being indifferent to personal identity per se. But that is compatible with those same rules being biased in favor of individual moral virtue, including giving to others in some circumstances, because virtue is something which can generally be acquired by individuals, whoever they happen to be, through their own efforts. More generally, see William Galston, "Liberal Virtues," *American Political Science Review* 82 (1988): 1277–1290.

82. For an introduction to the relevant legislation as it exists now, see, for example, Edward Jay Beckwith and Jana DeSirgh, "Tax Law and Private Foundations," in Odendahl, ed., *America's Wealthy,* pp. 267–293; Clotfelter, *Impact of Tax Reform;* Clotfelter, *Federal Tax Policy and Charitable Giving* (Chicago: University of Chicago Press, 1985); and John Simon, "The Tax Treatment of Nonprofit Organizations: A Review of Federal and State Policies," in Powell, ed., *The Nonprofit Sector,* pp. 67–98.

83. "Mr. Carnegie's 'Gospel of Wealth,'" Hendrick, ed., *Miscellaneous Writings,* p. 135.

84. For further discussion of the features of what I call a "liberal character" in the context of Mill's thought, see J. Riley, *Liberal Utilitarianism,* especially Part II.

85. Mill, "On Liberty," John Stuart Mill, *Collected Works,* vol. 18, p. 263.

_____ a Businessman's Philanthropic Creed

A CENTENNIAL PERSPECTIVE ON CARNEGIE'S "GOSPEL OF WEALTH"

KENNETH FOX

When Andrew Carnegie's two essays "Wealth" and "The Best Fields for Philanthropy," appeared in the *North American Review* in 1889, he had not yet initiated the philanthropic ventures for which we remember him today: the libraries, the Peace Endowment, the Foundation for the Advancement of Teaching, and the Carnegie Corporation of New York. He was not recognized as a philanthropist or as someone with important ideas about charitable giving. Yet in 1955, when the Russell Sage Foundation funded a conference at Princeton University on the history of philanthropy in the United States, the participants agreed that the publication of Carnegie's essays was a major event in the chronology of that history.[1]

"Possession," it is said, "is nine-tenths of the law," and Carnegie's views were of interest because of the fantastic wealth he possessed. It was William T. Stead of the *Pall Mall Gazette* in London who when he reprinted the first essay changed the title to "The Gospel of Wealth." Stead hoped to scandalize his readers; "Gospel of Wealth" implied "Gospel of Mammon." Stead was probably disgusted when Carnegie took the revised title as a compliment and used it proudly for his own reprintings.[2]

Carnegie's innovation in these essays was to connect philanthropy with individual wealth, and specifically with the incredible fortunes of the new industrialists, the men Carnegie loved to refer to as his "fellow millionaires." His opening statement, "The problem of our age is the proper administration of wealth," announced a very different view of philanthropy from those prevailing at the time.

The chief function of philanthropy in 1889 was to aid in defining and enforcing the moral order of society. Carnegie was a businessman, and men who limited themselves to business were not appropriate guardians of the moral order. In describing Carnegie's two essays as a *businessman's creed,* I emphasize that they were an iconoclastic view. When we commemorate the centennial of Carnegie's "Gospel," we are acknowledging the importance of the essays at the time they were written, and also the steadily expanding importance to philanthropy of business, business people and business wealth over the intervening century.

I. Mid-Nineteenth Century Philanthropy and the Businessman

The innovative character of Carnegie's "Gospel" can best be appreciated by contrasting it with the reception of another very important document in the history of American philanthropy: the Last Will and Testament of Stephen Girard. Like Carnegie, Girard was a businessman who accumulated a fortune of exceptional proportions. Although the absolute amounts—somewhat in excess of $5 million—do not seem large today, Girard was probably the wealthiest individual in America at the time of his death in 1831. He owned the largest private bank in Philadelphia, was a prominent international merchant, owned hundreds of buildings and pieces of land in and around his native Philadelphia, and was an early developer of the anthracite coal fields of eastern Pennsylvania.

Like Carnegie in 1889, Girard was not known as a philanthropist. One of the popular biographies appearing soon after his death explained that business was more than his profession, it was "a passion." He had "the touch of Midas, . . . in his hands . . . every thing was turned into gold."[3] By mid-nineteenth century philanthropic principles, Girard's obsession with business and the accumulation of wealth was undesirable and potentially detrimental. While he lived, Girard gave not a clue about his intentions for the disposition of his fortune. The potential for harm to the social order of Philadelphia, if his distributions proved unwise, was immense. Hence the great anxiety about the contents of his Will, and the great significance attached to it once its provisions became known.

Philanthropy in mid-nineteenth century America was supervised and dominated by the unitary elites in cities, towns, and counties. Although leading businessmen and men of wealth in Philadelphia and other cities were almost always part of the elite group, wealth alone was not a basis for acceptance. Social standing and civic leadership were essential attributes, and also crucial responsibilities, for members of an elite. Elite membership was achieved and deserved on neither of these grounds, but rather because of *virtue*, often referred to as *republican virtue* to link it with the unique origins and destiny of the United States.[4]

The philanthropic activities of the elites included promulgating and enforcing standards of beneficence and charity, passing judgment on charitable behavior—or its lack—among the population, and financing and managing charitable institutions: primarily schools, hospitals and orphanages.

Stephen Girard had little interest in elite responsibilities. The best he could be commended for was his "personal philanthropy," a polite way of excusing his failings as a public figure. During the yellow fever epidemic of 1793, Girard had run the city's temporary hospital. As later biographers point out, however, Girard undertook supervision of the dying not for charity's sake, but rather to back up his assertion that yellow fever was not contagious. His aim was to prevent the epidemic from depressing business conditions in the city.[5]

By rights, Philadelphia's elite should have criticized Girard's behavior. His life presented an almost unmitigated example of obsession with business, neglect of public responsibilities, and greed. Fortuitously, and unexpectedly, the terms of his Will provided the guardians of Philadelphia's moral order a basis for reinterpreting his actions and intentions. Girard made modest bequests to some of his relatives and left nothing to others, a consequence of turmoil within the family. He freed his black slave, Hannah, and settled $200 a year upon her for life. He established perpetual funds of $30,000 for the Pennsylvania Hospital; $20,000 for the Pennsylvania Institute for the Deaf and Dumb; $10,000 for the purchase of fuel for the poor; $500,000 for the City of Philadelphia to improve streets and buildings in the dock district where he had made his fortune; and $300,000 for the Commonwealth of Pennsylvania to develop canals. Most prominently, he provided $2,000,000 to construct a college for the education of at least three hundred "poor male white orphan children," and made arrangements to cover its year-to-year operating expenses.

The Will provided the materials for resurrecting Girard's reputation through the argument that he had been a secret philanthropist who guarded his true motives. The text of the Will was published in a number of pamphlets, each appending a brief biography of Girard that imputed the necessary motives to him. Longer biographies appeared later. Henry W. Arey's biography emphasized that Girard was not motivated by love of money. Disappointments in his youth and an unhappy marriage "rendered business and the accumulation of wealth rather a necessary occupation than a source of delight."[6] "The accumulation of money was then the result, and not the aim of his labors;" and Arey quotes from one letter among Girard's private papers, "When I rise in the morning, my only effort is to labor so hard during the day, that when night comes, I may be enabled to sleep soundly";[7] and from another, "I live like a galley-slave, constantly occupied and often passing the night without sleeping. . . . I do not value fortune. The love of labor is my highest ambition."[8] Arey commended Girard's life to readers as "instructive" because "above all it exemplifies how the hard toil of a life-time, and the thirst for gold, may be elevated and sanctified by being devoted to the claims of humanity."[9]

Two other pamphlets offered similar reasoning. The biography in the pamphlet published by Thomas and Robert Desilver concluded that Girard deserved to be called a "PUBLIC BENEFACTOR" for the "PUBLIC OBJECTS" he addressed in his Will. These "proclaim him as one of the *first* PHILANTHROPISTS OF THE AGE." The biography praised Girard for devoting most of his fortune to "the BENEFIT OF THE COMMUNITY; and not the gratification of private passions, or individual avarice."[10]

The pamphlet publishing a speech by Job R. Tyson in January 1849, on the first anniversary of the founding of Girard College, also judged Girard as a philanthropist by his ends rather than his means. Tyson condemned "greedy accumulation" simply to glorify a benefactor's name.

> Yet if the one object of Girard's life, the end to which he dedicated his daily and midnight labors, was not the indulgence of voluptuous

appetite, but the establishment of a great public charity, he is re-
deemed from the imputation of a contracted spirit and an engrossing
selfishness. If, in addition to these, the plan of his beneficence be as
remarkable for wise and comprehensive sagacity, as for the magnificence of its income, he rises to the condition of a public benefactor.

Tyson's use of the conditional was particularly effective in pointing
out the essential moral.[11]

Three principles of mid-nineteenth century philanthropy are il-
lustrated by the posthumous treatment of Girard. First, the wealth
of men of large fortunes is only accumulated into their hands; they
are not creators of wealth. Accumulation is attributed to greed if
the motivation for it is selfish, or to innate nature that turns every
enterprise to money—the touch of Midas. Second, to deserve the
name of philanthropy, wealth must be applied to commendable
public purposes. Society shall be the judge of whether proper philanthropic ends have been achieved, and praise or condemn the
benefactor accordingly. And third, to deserve recognition as a philanthropist, one must have had in mind while accumulating one's
wealth a plan for the support of worthy public projects or the
creation of institutions beneficial to society.

The extravagant publicity given to Girard's Will, accompanied
by the contrived histories of his life and motives, functioned as a
guide and warning to other men of business who amassed great
fortunes. Whatever their actual motives while alive, they could put
themselves straight with society at death by distributing their estates
to approved charities and purposes, as Girard had done. Above
all, society, headed by the elite leaders of the community, remained
the guardian and arbiter of philanthropic activity. Maintaining the
moral order was the overarching objective, and it was essential to
prove that this had been Girard's chief objective as well, in life and
in his bequests.

II. Carnegie's Gospel of Wealth as a Businessman's Creed

Carnegie's essays of 1889 should be read as an attempt to revolu-
tionize mid-nineteenth century philanthropy. This was not the first
time Carnegie had published essays challenging conventional views.
Whether he is labeled a Social Darwinist or simply an Individualist,

Carnegie believed society progressed through the innovative contributions of talented individuals. To realize the progressive benefits, society must allow these talented individuals free reign to exercise their powers and imaginations. In two essays published in 1886, Carnegie had applied this philosophy to industrial relations between employers and their workers. The intersection of the essays with the upheavals of that year, the Eight Hour Movement and the Haymarket Affair, brought Carnegie considerable notoriety.[12]

The 1889 essays expanded the Individualist argument by suggesting that the talents of successful businessmen could be applied beneficially to fields beyond the realm of commerce and industry. This directly challenged the mid-nineteenth century pattern of elite dominance of the social order, and of philanthropy. Carnegie hoped to see society loosen the control of traditional, largely hereditary elites and pin its hopes for progress on the talented few—most, if not all, of whom would be businessmen like himself. It is in this spirit that the 1889 essays constitute a businessman's creed.

The two "Gospel of Wealth" essays were an attempt to overturn the prevailing principles on which charitable giving and philanthropic activities were organized. Carnegie began by challenging the principle that men of great fortunes were not responsible for creating the wealth they accumulate. Manufacturing and industrialization, he argued, driven forward by the laws of economic competition, had revolutionized society—providing cheap goods on a mass scale that made ordinary people richer and more comfortable than the masters and the princes of past times. This revolution had come about only because "great scope" had been allowed "for the exercise of special ability in the merchant and in the manufacturer who has to conduct affairs upon a great scale."[13] The talent for managing large enterprises was rare. As great enterprises succeeded, they inevitably realized large profits, which flowed into the hands of the men of talent who organized and managed them. Therefore, Carnegie concluded: "It is a law . . . that men possessed of this peculiar talent for affairs, under the free play of economic forces must, of necessity, soon be in receipt of more revenue than can be judiciously expended upon themselves."[14]

Next Carnegie challenged the second principle: that society is the arbiter of what is beneficent, philanthropic and in the public interest. He allowed very little role for society to weigh and judge

philanthropic schemes. Instead, he argued that just as society benefited from the commercial and industrial ventures of men of exceptional talent, it could achieve the greatest benefit from the
surplus wealth that flowed into their hands by allowing them to
administer it for public purposes. Manufacturers and merchants
who amassed great fortunes must be given a free hand in disbursing
their wealth. Their exceptional talents guaranteed they would discover and pursue the philanthropic uses most beneficial to society.

As for the third principle, that the motives of the man of wealth
while alive must have been appropriately philanthropic for him to
be proclaimed a public benefactor at his death, Carnegie offered a
more aggressive strategy: The true philanthropist must turn his surplus to beneficial ends during his lifetime; otherwise society would
lose the benefit of his exceptional talents as a manager of wealth.
Carnegie attacked the practice of those—like Girard—who distributed none of their surplus for public purposes until death. Although
some posthumous bequests succeeded, "the cases are not few in
which the real object sought by the testator is not attained, nor are
they few in which his real wishes are thwarted." The ability to manage wealth "so as to be really beneficial to the community," Carnegie
argued, is no less exceptional than the talent for amassing great fortunes. Men who waited until death to distribute their fortunes "may
fairly be thought men who would not have left [their wealth] at all
had they been able to take it with them. The memories of such cannot be held in grateful remembrance."[15]

The most important shifts away from mid-nineteenth century
philanthropic philosophy advocated in Carnegie's essays are the
principles that great fortunes amassed in business represent wealth
created for society by men of exceptional talent, and that responsibility for philanthropic distribution and administration of surplus
wealth arising from business should reside solely with the creators
of that wealth. In the statement most often repeated from these essays, Carnegie emphasized the *duty* of the man of wealth:

> to consider all surplus revenues which come to him simply as trust
> funds, which he is called upon to administer, and strictly bound as a
> matter of duty to administer in the manner which, in his judgment, is
> best calculated to produce the most beneficial results for the commu-
> nity—the man of wealth thus becoming the mere trustee and agent for

his poorer brethren, bringing to their service his superior wisdom, experience, and ability to administer, doing for them better than they would or could do for themselves.[16]

Most important to Carnegie in this passage is the phrase "in his judgment," behind which stands his Individualist or Social Darwinist philosophy of social progress. Carnegie hoped to free philanthropy from antiquated social standards and moral controls so that the imaginativeness of the successful businessman could flourish and also receive approbation as the best philanthropic management of society's wealth.

Compacted and codified, the argument in Carnegie's two essays becomes a call for great industrialists to assume leadership of charitable giving and the founding and managing of philanthropic institutions. Carnegie's hope was to win supporters for "scientific philanthropy," which he believed he was helping to initiate with his second essay:

> Those who have surplus wealth give millions every year which produce more evil than good, and really retard the progress of the people, because most of the forms in vogue to-day for benefiting mankind only tend to spread among the poor a spirit of dependence upon alms, when what is essential for progress is that they should be inspired to depend upon their own exertions.[17]

Much of Carnegie's notion of a scientific philanthropy also has its roots in business and industry. The proposals for dealing with the poor are derived from methods of personnel management Carnegie pioneered in his own factories.

Carnegie fervently believed that business and business people formed the vanguard of social progress and he undertook in these essays to explain their progressive responsibilities to them. Much of the historical importance of the "Gospel" derives from the response it elicited from business people, and from social reformers with whom they allied in the 1890s and the early twentieth century—the next subject we will consider.

III. The Businessman and the Social Reformer: Turn-of-the-Century Allies

Carnegie's blatant promotion of successful businessmen as the proper leaders of philanthropy escaped being roundly condemned because it corresponded with emerging reform ideas about society's problems and how to solve them. To readers of 1889, his views were recognizable as an extension of the approach to social melioration known as "the Social Question" or "the Labor Question." Formulated during the 1880s to explain the great Depression of the 1870s, and also the violence of industrial strikes and lockouts, the Social Question attributed both kinds of social upheaval to the increasingly unequal distribution of wealth inevitably brought about by the rise of industry. This tendency was considered most dangerous to the urban middle classes, which stood between industrial capital and labor but had no immediate role in industrial development, and thus no basis to appeal to either side for moderation. Magazines of informed middle class opinion, such as the *North American Review,* flourished on controversy over the nature of the Social Question and proposed schemes to confront it.[18]

Carnegie's essays took the form characteristic of "answers" to the Social Question designed to win sympathy from the educated, scientifically minded middle class to whom Darwinian evolution, and the new sociology encompassed by the term Social Darwinism, appealed. While many of these people disliked sharing purposes with powerful industrialists and men of enormous wealth, there were many who recognized that social reform could be strengthened by alliances with men like Carnegie, who espoused progressive objectives. Alternative responses to the increasing maldistribution of wealth, such as a federal income tax or Henry George's Single Tax, were sure to incite antagonism from the very wealthy. Also taxation involved expanding the role of the state and state-run institutions, which few in the middle class favored. From a practical point of view, if future industrial evolution were to involve further concentration of wealth in the hands of a small class of very powerful industrialists, cooperation between the possessors of great wealth and the middle class, with individual industrialists taking leadership roles, had considerable appeal. Many in the middle class were themselves business people. The kinds of philanthropic enterprises Carnegie recommended in the second essay—libraries, universities, scientific endeavors—were the sort most likely to enhance his popularity with the educated, scientifically oriented segment of the middle class.[19]

Carnegie's insistence on the businessman's philanthropic administration of his surplus wealth while he remained alive appealed to the reform-minded among the middle class, brightening the prospects for alliances between social activists and businessmen. Carnegie regarded business as the most important force for social improvement. His discussion of purposes in the second essay committed philanthropy to systematic efforts at improving society by changing it. Carnegie hoped to see philanthropy join with business in promoting the "progress of the race," a favorite term from his reading of the Social Darwinist literature.

In the period immediately following 1889, social reformers and reform organizations revolutionized American "charity," shifting philanthropic objectives and institutions onto a reform basis. Carnegie's insistence that businessmen with surplus wealth become involved in establishing and managing philanthropic enterprises helped create a favorable climate for modernizing charity and charitable organizations. Carnegie's "Gospel" put the propertied leisure class of institutional board members on the defensive by implying they were more intent on holding fast to their control and prerogatives than on serving the best interest of society. Displacing these conservative elements from their positions of power was a crucial step in the struggle for reform.

Charity reform and other social, economic, and political reforms associated with the "Progressive Era" from the late 1890s to the end of World War I advanced through cooperation between reform activists and forward-looking people in business. Inherited or landed wealth as the source of philanthropic giving rapidly declined in importance. Business, particularly large industrial and financial enterprises, became the dominant source of philanthropic and charitable funds, and businessmen—and a few businesswomen—assumed active roles as givers, administrators, and leaders of philanthropy. Carnegie's 1889 essay acquired a far-seeing prescience as change unfolded in patterns he had advocated.[20]

IV. The Businessman's Creed in the Age of the Corporation

Carnegie wrote his essays in an era of family business, when the corporate form of business enterprise was in an early stage. He addressed his creed for the distribution and administration of wealth to people who amassed their wealth in sole proprietorships, or partnerships among family and friends. Individual and family business people, interested in social leadership and philanthropic activity, found Carnegie's creed inspiring and helpful. No institutional barriers separated them from the profits of their enterprises; their business wealth was their own, to do with as they willed. But as business institutions altered radically during the 1890s and the early twentieth century, Carnegie's principles became more difficult to translate into action. Without reinterpretation, the relevance of the "Gospel of Wealth" for twentieth century corporate business would be merely historical.

Carnegie's philanthropic philosophy remained prominent as the corporate form of business enterprise rose to dominate the American economy, but his principles were difficult to apply to corporate creators and administrators of wealth. It is customary to link Carnegie's essays with the emergence of the philanthropic foundation, which introduced the bureaucratic methods of the corporation to charitable giving and administration. Carnegie was antagonistic to the corporate form for his own business enterprises. Following retirement from active management in 1900, Carnegie devoted himself to philanthropic ventures, but he remained ambivalent about corporate organization. John D. Rockefeller and Margaret Olivia Slocum Sage—Russell Sage's widow—were the originators of the modern foundation. Only out of frustration with other methods of disbursing his wealth did Carnegie establish a corporation with general philanthropic purposes—the Carnegie Corporation of New York.[21]

Carnegie's ambivalence about the corporate form of organization, whether for a business or philanthropic entity, was a reaction to its tendency to diffuse responsibility among salaried managers and dissipate the incentives for imaginative thinking and creative innovation. Carnegie doubted a corporate bureaucracy could be a force for social progress, either in creating wealth or in administering it for philanthropic ends. Converting his own vast wealth, or that of Sage or Rockefeller, into a perpetual capital fund controlled by a bureaucratic foundation was only a marginal improvement over Girard's posthumous endowment of a college for orphans. Where were the sparks of creative imagination to come from once the original benefactor was dead and out of the way?[22]

The essence of Carnegie's creed is his insistence that the *creators* of society's wealth are the proper leaders of its philanthropic activities, and that they must exercise leadership while they are alive and at the height of their powers. In the twentieth-century context, where business corporations dominate the economy, this means that Carnegie would expect corporations and corporate executives to assume the lead in philanthropic giving and administration. Only they, with their experience in creating economic prosperity, possess the abilities beneficial philanthropic management demands.

How have twentieth-century corporations and corporate executives confronted these responsibilities? The first generation of corporate businessmen tended to extract personal wealth from the corporation and engage in philanthropic activities along the same lines as independent business people, involving the corporation only under special circumstances. Julius Rosenwald financed his well-known philanthropic endeavors from the fortune he amassed through dividends on Sears, Roebuck stock—he reputedly owned more than 90 percent of the shares. Rosenwald initiated only two philanthropic innovations within the corporation: the Agricultural Foundation, which grew out of his offer in 1912 to give $1,000 to any county that would raise the additional money required to employ a trained agricultural expert; and the Employee's Savings and Profit Sharing Pension Fund, which benefited only Sears employees and their families. Rosenwald did not envision Sears, Roebuck, or other corporations, becoming leaders in charitable giving and philanthropy.[23]

The philosophy of the corporation's responsibilities to society during the first part of the century was best expressed by Edward A. Filene, the department store magnate: "Nine-tenths of a businessman's best public service can be rendered by the way he conducts his business."[24] Filene was referring to the new forms of employee relations corporations were initiating, from recreation and health programs, through the "Sociological Department" at Ford Motor Company, to so-called corporate paternalism as exemplified by the Endicott-Johnson Shoe Company and National Cash Register. This approach to social improvement looked forward to a job with a corporation for every citizen, and the provision of social services within the corporate employment relationship. Filene's brother, A. Lincoln Filene, elaborated the implications for philanthropy in his 1924 book *A Merchant's Horizon:*

Business cares about its obligations. . . . And yet business remains

business. It has not gone into charity. . . . Business has proved to
itself that the making of money and the making of citizens not only
can, but must, go on together, for the simple reason that neither
process can solvently function without the other. For too long a time
the problem of human betterment was looked upon as a side issue,
a charity, subsisting on the doles of philanthropists. Now it is being
put where it belongs—on a business basis, in business itself.[25]

The Filenes and the many corporate leaders who shared their
views did not intend to disparage philanthropic activity by foundations and private individuals. Their philosophy concerned the
role the corporation should play in social progress. They believed
the corporation should retain its surplus wealth within the business
to enrich employment conditions and the lives of its employees. As
these conditions improved, and as more and more people entered
corporate employment, society would advance and its problems
would be ameliorated.

The idea that the corporation should attempt to act like a philanthropist, giving away its earnings to charitable organizations
and deserving causes, was not directly contemplated. The problem
with the corporation pursuing philanthropic ends was that a corporation is an artificial individual. Its bureaucratic hierarchies of
professional managers and technicians could achieve rationality in
managing its business affairs through competition and the pursuit
of returns on invested capital. As a citizen of society, however,
intent on administering its surplus wealth for socially beneficial
ends, the business corporation had no basis for formulating objectives and rationalizing its actions.

The rationale for corporate philanthropy had to be built up; it
could not be fashioned out of whole cloth. In specific instances
where corporations were able to conceive beneficial outcomes for
themselves *as corporations,* they did enter into charitable and philanthropic activities. Railroads became major supporters of the
YMCA in the late nineteenth century because their numerous tran-
sient employees could greatly benefit from the YMCA's services. A
nationwide network of "Railroad YMCAs" provided rooms, meals,
and recreational activities to railroad workers away from their
homes on long runs. During World War I, corporations gave company funds to the War Drives and contributed to the Red Cross.
In the 1920s, corporations and corporate executives became prom-

inently involved in the Community Chests. They explained this activity in terms of giving something back to the communities in which they operated and in which their employees resided. Corporations also experimented with the establishment of company foundations similar to the foundations created by individuals with their personal wealth.[26]

Another promising experiment involved corporate executives and managerial personnel taking a personal interest in the local communities where the corporation had establishments. As early as 1914, Thomas J. Watson initiated a community service policy at IBM:

> We want you to take time off from IBM to do a good job as citizens because communities will only be as good as the citizens make them. We want IBM to be a real part of the citizenship of this country and the world. Keep that in mind. That is one of your duties. We are trying to develop not only IBM and develop people for IBM, but we are trying to help in our small way to develop this great country of ours.[27]

Corporations urged management people to be active in churches, organizations, social welfare agencies and local government—to provide a sense that the corporation was doing its part in shouldering the community's problems and guiding its development. Many corporate managers who began their careers in the 1920s and 1930s took these responsibilities very seriously and looked back with great satisfaction later in life upon their community involvement.

The corporation's difficulties in defining its relationship to society were not confined to charitable giving and community involvement. The business side of the corporation raised social questions as well. In 1932, Adolf Berle and Gardiner Means posed the issues in compelling fashion in their book, *The Modern Corporation and Private Property*.[28] The problem as they saw it was that the management of the corporation had become divorced from its ownership. Owners were little more than impersonal holders of stock certificates who placed all responsibility in the hands of salaried professionals with little or no ownership interest. Stockholder democracy was unworkable as a managerial procedure, leaving it up to the corporate managers to define business and social objectives. The crucial question for Berle and Means was whether the managers ought to be trusted with powers and responsibilities affecting all aspects of American life. Upon what basis were managers to decide how the corporation should participate in society, and to what ends?

Before progress was made in addressing these questions, the corporation's involvements became even more complex. The first and second versions of the National Recovery Administration embroiled them in cooperation with government to alleviate the Depression of the 1930s, and World War II brought partnerships with government in war production. After the war, corporate expansion formed the core of American efforts at reconstruction in Europe, Japan, and elsewhere around the globe. By the 1950s, most large corporations had entered into formal and informal partnerships with government involving national defense and international political objectives that required them to organize and carry out activities extending far beyond the pursuit of profits through the production of goods and services.

The attempt to resolve these dilemmas took the form of the "corporate social responsibility" movement. Around 1950, many corporate managers and business experts began using the notion of the social responsibilities of the corporation to rationalize—and explain to the public—the way companies ran their businesses and conducted themselves as "citizens" of society. Most expressions of corporate social responsibility encouraged corporations to act as leaders, pointing the way toward progress and applying their productive and organizational capabilities to move society forward.

In assuming responsibility for social leadership, corporations would naturally shoulder leadership responsibilities in the field of philanthropy as well. Richard Eells, a consultant to General Electric and a forceful advocate of corporate social responsibility, wrote in his 1956 book *Corporation Giving in a Free Society,*

> Philanthropy has a long and noble history, extending through many centuries and reaching into all countries. In the free American environment it has become stamped with a corporate character; and the rapid contemporary growth of corporation giving promises a new era in the long evolution of philanthropic work. . . . We have reached

a stage in the evolution of corporate enterprise and the development of philanthropy where the two are meeting. The corporation has become a philanthropic force in the sheer bulk of its contributions. It has yet, however, to establish itself as a leader in philanthropic endeavor. The reason for this lag is not merely the newness of the development. It lies rather in the failure to formulate a doctrinal basis for such leadership.[29]

The doctrine of philanthropic leadership might have taken shape in the wake of Eells's and others' writings, if corporate social responsibility had firmly established itself. This was not to be. On close examination, the new philosophy raised questions of power, legitimacy, and democracy that could not be answered satisfactorily. Corporations acquired their power through their economic functions—organizing production, providing employment, and creating society's prosperity and wealth. If this power were now to be turned toward social objectives, the first consequence would be to elevate whoever controlled decision-making within the corporation to a position of tremendous influence over the character and the direction of national social change. What was the constitutional and political basis for such power? How could corporate social power, however responsibly exercised, be made compatible with democratic notions of a society of free individuals, all equal in their influence over their collective fate?

The most telling critiques of corporate social responsibility were those elaborating the lack of a basis for corporation managers to choose social objectives for the corporation to pursue, or to decide what amounts of effort to commit. In a 1959 article that harked back to Carnegie's rhetoric in the "Gospel," Eugene Rostow of Yale Law School asked,

> Should [the socially responsible corporation] regard its residual profits, not as "belonging to" its stockholders in some ultimate sense, but as a pool of funds to be devoted in considerable part to the public interest, as the directors conceive it—to hospitals, parks, and charities in the neighborhood of its plants; to the local symphony or the art museum; to scholarships for the children of employees, or to other forms of support for the educational system of the nation at large? If what is good for the country is good for General Motors, as is indeed the case, does this view of managerial responsibility set

any limit upon the directors' discretion in spending corporate funds for what they decide is the public good?[30]

In the face of this and other lines of attack, corporations and corporate executives who had championed social responsibility drew back from the limelight of publicity. Practical difficulties bedeviled them as well. Corporate social responsibility set a higher standard of corporate behavior than most professional managers wished to maintain. Particularly damaging to the social responsibility movement was the exposure and conviction of executives of General Electric and other major electrical equipment and appliance manufacturers for conspiring to fix prices and divide up markets during the 1950s. General Electric had been a leader in the social responsibility movement and in encouraging corporate leadership in philanthropy. Ralph Cordiner, GE's chairman, denied any knowledge of the conspiratorial activities of his subordinates, raising fatal doubts about either his truthfulness or his sincerity.[31] If corporate executives could not be trusted to follow basic economic and legal rules of competition, how could the public be expected to entrust them with social responsibility and philanthropic leadership?

V. The Corporation, and Corporate Philanthropic Involvement, in Crisis

Following the debacle of social responsibility in the late 1950s, corporations retreated from advocating leadership roles for themselves in the realm of philanthropy and charitable giving. Yet corporate contributions quietly grew. Today, the rate of contributions stands at an all-time high and corporate interest in philanthropic activity is increasing. If Andrew Carnegie could return, he would be excited by the level of corporate involvement and exasperated by the reluctance of corporations and corporate business people to promulgate a philosophy explaining their actions.

In place of a positive creed, companies presently explain their philanthropic involvement in terms of "enlightened corporate self-interest"—a corporation should engage in philanthropic activity because the benefits to society will benefit the corporation itself in the long run. The practical workings of enlightened corporate self-interest place the corporation in the passive stance of being besieged by an overwhelming deluge of requests, pressures and demands. The initiative lies with those seeking corporate support. Company policies for philanthropic involvement under the enlightened self-interest approach take the form of guidelines for deciding which requests to honor and in what amounts. International Harvester (now Navistar) commented on its recent policy update:

> Our planning for a revised set of philanthropic priorities began with the premise that since there is a virtually endless number of legitimate, worthwhile philanthropic needs and organizations dealing with them, IH's philanthropy should have a clear relationship with the goals and interests of the Corporation.[32]

Enlightened corporate self-interest would aid corporate managers in making decisions if they were able to clearly formulate the interests of their corporations. Increasingly, they cannot. John Kenneth Galbraith brought to light one part of the problem in his 1967 book *The New Industrial State,* by showing that profit maximization was not the objective toward which large corporations oriented their business affairs. Instead, Galbraith argued, corporations, government, and other large, influential organizations— including large philanthropic organizations—had come to form a "technostructure," controlled and operated by a common group of managerial people whom he designated "the planning class." These planning-minded organizers appeared to administer the institutions by which they were employed along independent lines, but their larger purposes as a class were to coordinate the economic, political, and social sectors of American society in the pursuit of long-term growth and cultural stability. The security and well-being of the planning class itself were important, but incidental, consequences of their success.[33]

Galbraith formulated his critique in the tradition of Berle and Means and the critics of corporate social responsibility, emphasizing the dilemmas and dangers of abdicating all responsibility for choosing and pursuing corporate objectives into the hands of a small class of professional managers—whatever their prestige and abilities as leading businessmen and businesswomen. Galbraith's analysis of planning class behavior suggested that a sense of social responsibility did in fact underlie their efforts. But having abandoned profit maximization as the primary basis for corporate business decision-making, how, Galbraith asked, could the new corporate managers be certain their guidance would eventuate in the best results for society as a whole?

Galbraith portrayed a planning class in confident control of corporations and other large institutions. Since the 1960s, control has become more volatile. Corporate wealth is increasingly conceptualized in terms of assets whose value is determined by the amount for which they can be sold. Hostile takeovers are organized to extract the most valuable assets and dispose of the remainder for whatever they will bring. The prize may be merely a brand name—Kool-Aid or Philadelphia Cream Cheese—that can be exploited more aggressively.[34]

The business corporation, and the corporate sector as a whole, are in crisis. The crisis arises from intimations that economic and financial organizations on a tremendously larger scale are possible. Developments in communications and computers are the most dramatic technological transformation since the electrical and chemical revolution of the 1890s and early 1900s. An optimistic outcome is by no means assured, but corporate anxiety derives from fears of underestimating the potential for change.

The immediate effects of the crisis upon corporate involvement in philanthropy have been positive. Corporate executives are recognizing the need to be more adventurous in all areas, philanthropy included. Carnegie would not be impressed, however. If he were here to survey the situation, he would be disgusted by the timidity of today's corporate executives—their reluctance to publicize their real objectives and debate the contributions of the corporation to social progress. With his love of creating a sensation, we can imagine Carnegie urging a corporation with billions in profits to limit stockholder dividends to a reasonable rate of return and declare the remainder "surplus wealth," to be distributed for philanthropic purposes at the discretion of the management.[35]

Carnegie's "Gospel of Wealth" was about the social creativity of the businessman, his exceptional talent for organization and the benefits society might derive from allowing those talents free reign. Carnegie's 1889 essays must not be read as a call for businessmen to turn to philanthropy as the place to begin doing good. Although he enjoyed playing philanthropist with the millions he took with him when he retired from business in 1900, Carnegie continued to believe that his best service to society had been performed as a steelmaker and employer of men. He saw the philanthropic arrangements and activities of 1889 retarding social progress and encouraged businessmen with surplus wealth to become involved in order to initiate much needed reform.

He would unquestionably make the same arguments today, acknowledging Filene's dictum from the 1920s as a paraphrase of his own philosophy: "Nine-tenths of a businessman's best public service can be rendered by virtue of the way he conducts business. . . ." Thus Carnegie would be distressed by attributions of altruism to a "non-profit" or "independent" sector, suggesting that the "profit" or business sector is not committed first and foremost to serving society's best interests. Business history has questioned Carnegie's methods and motives, but it does not endorse the popular assessment that Carnegie amassed profits ruthlessly in his business affairs and then turned to serving society only in his philanthropic guise.

How can we best commemorate Carnegie's essays a century after their publication? We can remember him as a businessman who believed that business is society's best hope for progress, and we can remember his belief that philanthropy was desperately in need of reform by men with business abilities. When we consider the "responsibilities of wealth" today, we should emphasize that these responsibilities adhere most immediately to those who create and control society's wealth: the businessmen and businesswomen of the corporations.

Notes

I am grateful to Peter Hall for suggestions of sources and examples from the history of corporate philanthropic activity, and for his careful reading and criticism of a draft of the paper. His overview of business and corporate charitable giving and involvement, "Business Giving and Social Investment in the United States," will appear in Richard Magat, ed., *American Philanthropy* (New York: Oxford University Press, in press).

1. Russell Sage Foundation, *Report of the Princeton Conference on the History of Philanthropy in the United States* (New York: Russell Sage Foundation, 1956), p. 15.

2. The first essay, "Wealth," originally appeared in the June 1889 issue of the *North American Review,* the second, "The Best Fields for Philan-

thropy," in the December 1889 issue. Stead later achieved notoriety as the author of *If Christ Came to Chicago,* an early attempt at "exposé." See Andrew Carnegie, *The Gospel of Wealth and Other Timely Essays,* ed. Edward C. Kirkland (Cambridge, Mass.: Harvard University Press, 1962), note on p. 14. Carnegie's two essays are also reprinted in this volume as "The Gospel of Wealth."

3. *The Will of the Late Stephen Girard, Esq., Procured from the Office for the Probate of Wills, with a Short Biography of His Life* (Philadelphia: Thomas and Robert Desilver, 1832), pp. iv, vii.

4. For an introduction to elites in eighteenth and nineteenth century America, see Peter Dobkin Hall, *The Organization of American Culture, 1700–1900, Private Institutions, Elites, and the Origins of American Nationality* (New York: New York University Press, 1982).

5. *The Will of . . . Stephen Girard,* p. v. Harry Emerson Wildes, *Lonely Midas, The Story of Stephen Girard* (New York: Farrar and Rinehart, 1943), pp. 118–131. Wildes failed to avoid becoming an apologist for Girard. An adequate biography of Girard remains to be written.

6. Henry W. Arey, *The Girard College and Its Founder, Containing the Biography of Mr. Girard* (Philadelphia: Sherman and Co., 1869), pp. 23–24.

7. Ibid., p. 24.

8. Ibid., p. 25.

9. Ibid., p. 5.

10. *The Will of . . . Stephen Girard,* p. viii.

11. Job R. Tyson, *Discourse Delivered on the First Anniversary of The Girard College for Orphans . . .* (Philadelphia: Crissy & Markley, 1849), p. 4.

12. Andrew Carnegie, "An Employer's View of the Labor Question," published in the *Forum,* April 1886, and "Results of the Labor Struggle," *Forum,* August 1886. The Eight Hour Movement held demonstrations nationwide on May 1, 1886, which became the First of May still celebrated in much of the world as the international day of labor. The modern American Labor Day, in September, was established to divert attention from May 1, with its socialist and internationalist associations. The bombing central to the Haymarket Affair occurred on May 4, 1886. Carnegie's 1886 essays are reprinted in the collection edited by Kirkland; see above, note 2.

13. Carnegie, "Gospel of Wealth," in Kirkland, ed. *Gospel of Wealth,* p. 17.

14. Ibid., p. 17.

15. Ibid., p. 21. The idea of distributing one's surplus wealth while alive was probably impressed upon Carnegie by a pamphlet by the wealthy abolitionist and radical reformer Lewis Tappan, "Is It Right to Be Rich?" (New York: Anson D. F. Randolph & Co., 1869).

Carnegie backed up this facet of his creed by approving the trend toward stiffer inheritance taxes, graduated as high as 50% on great fortunes. He wrote: "Men who continue hoarding great sums all their lives, the proper use of which for public ends would work good to the community from which it chiefly came, should be made to feel that the community, in the form of the State, cannot thus be deprived of its proper share. By taxing estates heavily at death the State marks its condemnation of the selfish millionaire's unworthy life." "Gospel of Wealth," in Kirkland, ed., *Gospel of Wealth,* p. 22.

16. Carnegie, "Gospel of Wealth," p. 25.

17. Ibid., p. 32. Carnegie did not differ from men like Stephen Girard in terms of desire for power and control over vast wealth; what was unique about Carnegie was his belief in industry and commerce, and in men of exceptional business ability, as forces for social progress. Men like Girard avoided large charitable grants during their lifetimes out of reluctance to relinquish control of any part of their wealth. Carnegie believed that a much better means of control in life, and also after one's demise, was to use charitable ventures as an alternative to struggling to reinvest surplus profits and wealth in additional business undertakings. George Bernard Shaw provided a similar gospel for the industrialist Andrew Undershaft to use in convincing his daughter that progressive capitalism can save souls more effectively than Salvation Army revivalism. Shaw's play *Major Barbara,* written in 1905, was tremendously popular with American audiences.

18. The leading proponent of the Social Question was the statistician Carroll Wright, who served as the first U.S. Commissioner of Labor. An excellent biography and introduction to Wright's social analysis is James Leiby, *Carroll Wright and Labor Reform: The Origin of Labor Statistics* (Cambridge, Mass.: Harvard University Press, 1960).

19. Edward Kirkland has written a fascinating book describing late nineteenth century businessmen and their relation to society, which includes a discussion of the reception of Carnegie's "Gospel": *Dream and Thought in the Business Community, 1860–1900* (Ithaca: Cornell University Press, 1956).

20. The classic study of businessmen and turn-of-the-century reform is Robert Wiebe, *Businessmen and Reform* (Cambridge, Mass.: Harvard University Press, 1962).

21. John M. Glenn, Lillian Brandt, and F. Emerson Andrews, *Russell Sage Foundation, 1907–1946,* 2 vols. (New York: Russell Sage Foundation, 1947). An interesting memoir of Rockefeller's activities and the early years of the Rockefeller Foundation is Frederick Taylor Gates, *Chapters in My Life* (New York: Free Press, 1977).

22. The place to begin any study of Carnegie is Joseph Frazier Wall, *Andrew Carnegie* (New York: Oxford University Press, 1970). Wall writes: "With the creation of the Carnegie Corporation of New York in 1911, Carnegie had been forced to abandon almost all of the basic tenets of philanthropy he had expressed in the 'Gospel of Wealth.' . . . the creation of this vast philanthropic corporation under the most vague stipulations

was an open admission by Carnegie that a fortune as large as his could not possibly be administered and dispersed by a single man, no matter how 'superior his wisdom'" (p. 883).

23. Boris Emmet and John E. Jeuck, *Catalogues and Counters, A History of Sears, Roebuck and Company* (Chicago: University of Chicago Press, 1950), on the Agricultural Foundation, pp. 622–626. They report the Foundation was under the authority of the general advertising manager and was organized on a "for profit" basis. On the Savings and Profit Sharing Pension Fund, see M. R. Werner, *Julius Rosenwald, The Life of a Practical Humanitarian* (New York: Harper and Brothers, 1939), pp. 150–164.

24. Morrell Heald, *The Social Responsibilities of Business, Company and Community, 1900–1960* (Cleveland: The Press of Case Western Reserve University, 1970), p. 105.

25. Heald, *Social Responsibilities of Business,* p. 105, quoting from A. Lincoln Filene, *A Merchant's Horizon* (Boston: Houghton Mifflin, 1924), p. 258.

26. Heald, *Social Responsibilities of Business,* chapter 1 on the YMCAs and chapter 5 on the Community Chests. F. Emerson Andrews, *Corporation Giving* (New York: Russell Sage Foundation, 1952), provides a concise history of corporate involvement with the Y's, the War Drives, the Red Cross, and the Community Chests in chapter 2, "How Giving Grew."

27. Andrews, *Corporation Giving,* pp. 122–123.

28. Adolf A. Berle, Jr., and Gardiner C. Means, *The Modern Corporation and Private Property* (New York: Macmillan, 1932).

29. Richard Eells, *Corporation Giving in a Free Society* (New York: Harper and Brothers, 1956), pp. 1–3.

30. Eugene V. Rostow, "To Whom and For What Ends Is Corporate Management Responsible?" in Edward S. Mason, ed., *The Corporation In Modern Society* (Cambridge, Mass.: Harvard University Press, 1959); Atheneum edition, pp. 46–71; pp. 63–64.

31. Heald, *Social Responsibilities of Business,* p. 289. John Grant Fuller, *The Gentleman Conspirators* (New York: Grove Press, 1962). Heald's chapter 10 is an extended discussion of the "new" corporate responsibility of the 1950s. A more individualized approach to social responsibility can be found in Howard R. Bowen, *Social Responsibilities of the Businessman* (New York: Harper, 1953): "We cannot interpret the motives of businessmen solely in terms of profit maximization. The businessman is a person. He lives in society and shares the values and attitudes of that society. He wants to be liked. He wants to do what is expected of him— to be a success in terms of the currently accepted standards of success. He is keenly aware of the pressures on him, especially those emanating from labor, public opinion, and government. He has become deeply concerned about the human problems of business, as distinct from the purely pecuniary problems. He recognizes increasingly that his own long-run self-interest calls for the adjustment of his policies and actions with a regard for their social effects" (p. 116).

32. Benjamin Lord, *Corporate Philanthropy in America: New Perspectives for the Eighties* (Washington, D.C.: Taft Corporation, 1984), p.9.

33. John Kenneth Galbraith, *The New Industrial State,* 3d ed., rev. (New York: New American Library, 1978); originally published in 1967.

34. L. J. Davis, "Philip Morris's Big Bite," *New York Times Magazine,* Sunday, April 9, 1989.

35. An overview of current corporate philanthropic activity is Michael Useem, "Corporate Philanthropy," in Walter W. Powell, ed., *The Nonprofit Sector, A Research Handbook* (New Haven: Yale University Press, 1987), pp. 340–359.

Jane Addams's Views on the Responsibilities of Wealth

LOUISE W. KNIGHT

The title of this paper is in a sense offered tongue in cheek. While the theme of this book, "The Responsibilities of Wealth," captures a point of view held by Andrew Carnegie and other late nineteenth century philanthropists, it does not reflect the view of their contemporary, Jane Addams. She rejected the belief that an individual's wealth defined his or her responsibilities to the poor. Herself a woman of inherited wealth, Addams gave careful thought to the moral aspect of the relations between the classes, but her conclusions went in another direction.

A better phrase to describe Addams's views might be "the responsibilities of being human." In her life's work as the head of the Chicago settlement house, Hull House, as a national leader in social reform, and as a world leader for peace, she tried to honor the Judeo-Christian tenet that every individual merits equal respect. Her reform agenda thus rejected distinctions based on class and race and promoted social justice. She saw the gap between the ideal of equality and the reality, a gap even larger in her day than in our own, and fought to narrow it.

Her ideas about philanthropy were built on this philosophical foundation. Without denying the usefulness of money to accomplish good work, she rejected the materialism that overvalued such achievements. She sought, along with her colleagues in the settlement house movement, to instigate a "new philanthropy" by calling for the creation of cross-class social relations as a means to motivate people to desire the improvement of society.[1] Diverse social relations, Addams believed, would also bring benefits to the individual. In particular, they would benefit the wealthy, who lived in the greatest isolation from other classes.

Addams's claim that philanthropy would benefit the philanthropist was not new. Traditional philanthropy, while stressing the benefits to the poor as its first motive, acknowledged that the rich would gain in virtue from the encounter. This was based on the condescending assumption that the rich were morally superior to the poor. Uninterested in questions of sin and virtue and uncomfortable with assumptions of class superiority, Addams made a different case—that through cross-class relations philanthropists could gain knowledge of themselves and the common humanity that they shared with the poor. They could also improve their philanthropy.

Not surprisingly, she developed these ideas out of her own experience. As a single woman, she found that a life consisting of the company of family and friends and regular doses of cultural enrichment was too narrow, leaving her feeling isolated and dissatisfied with her uselessness and ignorance of the broader human world. Her first reason for founding Hull House, she always said, was to enrich her own life and give it meaning. Her desire to help the poor, also strong, came second in her mind. The benefits were to be mutual. Once she came to understand her own needs, she made it part of her life's work to guide others of wealth to make the same discoveries.

I. Class Differences

It is no coincidence that Addams founded Hull House and Carnegie published his essay "Wealth" in the same year, 1889. The decade of the 1880s had seen a rising concern in both England and the United States about the distance between the classes and the misery of the poor. Stimulated in part by such books as Henry George's influential *Progress and Poverty* (1879), citizens of these countries viewed the intensifying forces of industrialization on both sides of the Atlantic and the mounting wave of European emigration to the United States as developments which required new approaches. The period was, in Addams's words, one of "widespread moral malaise in regard to existing social conditions."[2] Carnegie and Addams each attempted to respond in his or her own way with a new theory of philanthropy.

Like others, Addams was deeply troubled by the gulf between the classes. The gulf was material, of course, but it was also social. In both England and the United States in the 1880s, the rich (and the middle classes) and the poor viewed each other with hostility. Then, as now, the rich scorned the poor for their lack of moral fiber. For their part, the poor hated the rich for their greed and lack of compassion. In his novel *Sybil, or Two Nations,* Benjamin Disraeli, England's prime minister when the decade of the eighties opened, characterized this gulf of understanding in vivid terms. The rich and poor, he said, "are as ignorant of each other's habits, thoughts, and feelings, as if they were dwellers in different zones or inhabitants of different planets."[3]

Acknowledging the existence of class differences has always made Americans uncomfortable. In Jane Addams's day, when the upper class felt confident enough in their moral superiority to the "lower class" to call it by that name, this discomfort was still felt. "We do not like to acknowledge," she wrote, "that Americans are divided into 'two nations,' as her prime minister once admitted of England, . . . even if we make that assumption the preface to a plea that the superior class has duties to the inferior."[4]

Class was a confusing riddle for Addams. While she inherited wealth, she was the daughter of a self-made man who had arrived on the Illinois frontier with few resources. Although her small hometown in the northern part of the state had a class structure (her father soon became the richest man in town), it was egalitarian in spirit. The culture she absorbed in school was imbued with class prejudices, but her family history taught her that class was an achieved status and that any superiority it brought with it was also achieved. For Addams, as an inheritor of wealth rather than the creator of it, the question was how to merit the wealth her father had earned.

II. The Years Leading to Hull House

Addams wrestled with this question during the eight years between her graduation from college and her bold act of founding Hull

House. Her first plan had been to care for the poor through a career in medicine. The year after her graduation from college, despite her father's unexpected death, she enrolled at the Woman's Medical College in Philadelphia, but her own health failed, forcing her to withdraw.

The loss of her only career goal left her vulnerable to the "family claim," as she was later to describe it. Yet the life of culture, wide reading, and travel that the family claim imposed on her also appealed to her, feeding as it did her love of learning. With her stepmother's full approval, she pursued a life of family visits and travel abroad. She was the perfect daughter of the upper class.

As the years passed, she became increasingly unhappy. Her education had given her high ideals of service but her life offered no outlet for their expression. The difficulty, she finally formulated, was "the assumption that the sheltered, educated girl has nothing to do with the bitter poverty and the social maladjustment which is all about her, and which, after all, cannot be concealed, for it breaks through poetry and literature in a burning tide which overwhelms her; it peers at her in the form of heavy-laden market women and underpaid street laborers, gibing her with a sense of her uselessness."[5]

Adding to her misery was her inability to find a way to express her sense of "human fellowship."[6] From her experience, sympathetic temperament, and wide reading, she was developing the conviction that, as one of her favorite authors, George Eliot, put it, "human nature is lovable."[7] In his essay on "Man the Reformer," another of Addams's favorite authors, Ralph Waldo Emerson, pointed out the missed opportunities: "See this wide society of laboring men and women," he wrote. "We allow ourselves to be served by them, we live apart from them and meet them without salute in the streets. We do not greet their talents, nor rejoice in their good fortune, nor foster their hopes."[8]

Other authors she read—Mazzini, Ruskin, Arnold—were imbued with this same ideal of the lovability of human nature, as was the philosophy of positivism, which she encountered in Comte's works. Yet, in the end, it was the idea's original source, the faith of the early Christians, that inspired her the most and Christ who became her model. In 1887, she returned to Italy to undertake a study of the Catacombs.[9] A year after founding Hull House, she was to write, "It seems simple to many of us to search for the Christ that is in each man and to found our likeness on Him—to believe in the brotherhood of all men because we believe in His."[10]

During this second trip, as she traveled and watched people from all walks of life go by, she found herself wanting to act on these feelings of brotherhood. Still the rules of her class held her back. A waiter who brought her breakfast one morning at a hotel became the focus of her longing; her memory of the encounter became to her a symbol of her inability to bridge the class gulf: "You turn helplessly to the waiter [but] feel it would be almost grotesque to claim from him the sympathy you crave because civilization has placed you apart."[11]

As the clash between her ideals and her conduct intensified, she became even more "pitifully miserable."[12] In the end, she viewed her decision to found Hull House as, in part, an act of desperation. She had become disgusted with her life of culture and observation and determined to find a way "to learn from life itself."[13] She had decided that "whatever perplexities and discouragement concerning the life of the poor were in store for me, I should at least know something at first-hand and have the solace of daily activity."[14] She would also be free of the tyranny of the family claim and its emotionally closed world.

Her desire to help the poor, initially expressed in her application to medical school, remained. But that motive had been reshaped by the realization, reached over the eight years, that she also needed to help herself. She had decided that the poor had what she sought: generosity, gaiety, hospitality, courtesy, and kindness in their human relations with each other.[15] She knew that she had culture and organizing abilities to offer the poor; now she knew as well that they had much to offer her.

Ellen Starr, writing to her sister a few months before she and Addams moved into Hull House, stressed that point. "Jane's idea, which she puts very much to the front and on no account will give up, is that [the settlement] is more for the people who do it than for the other class. She has worked that out of her own experience and ill health."[16] As Addams put it, "the dependence of classes on each other is reciprocal."[17]

During this period, she read about Toynbee Hall in London, the world's first settlement house, and was drawn to its innovative approach to bringing the classes together in social relations. At Toynbee, middle and upper class college-educated young people, called residents, shared a comfortable home in a poor neighborhood, earning their livelihood during the day in the city and spending their free time getting to know their neighbors in the evenings and weekends. Clubs, classes, and cultural events grew out of these relations, in response to the needs of the neighborhood. Local political reform and union organizing soon followed. However, the philosophy of the settlement was not simply one of service. Toynbee's founder, Canon Barnett, stressed that the residents benefited as much from their social relations with their neighbors, as their neighbors benefited from knowing the residents.

This philosophy struck a chord in Addams. A visit to Toynbee Hall in 1888 convinced her that she wanted to found a settlement too. Here, at last, was something she could do. With her friend Ellen Starr, she moved to Hull House, a fine old mansion in a rundown district of Chicago, in September 1889. She was twenty-nine years old. She and Starr had no plan, but intended to get to know their neighbors and see what activities might evolve. Addams saw the settlement simply as "an effort . . . to insist that a life is not lived as it should be unless it comes in contact with all kinds of people. We should endeavor, in addition to our individual and family [lives], to live a life that will bring us into a larger existence, and connect us with society as a whole."[18]

III. The Humanity of the Poor

As she met and talked with the working poor, her neighbors, she listened carefully, trying, as she later advised Hull House residents, to "empty her mind" of preconceived ideas and to truly learn what the lives of her neighbors were like.[19] The stories were gripping. She heard terrible tales of small children crippled by accidents that occurred when they were home alone while their mothers were at work. One had fallen out of a third story window, another had been burned. A third had a curved spine from being tied to the leg of the kitchen table, no doubt to keep him from burning himself or falling out of the window.[20]

She learned of the pressures on those who could find no regular employment and no steady income. When one man, who Addams knew had been able to earn only twenty-eight dollars in the preceding nine months and was thirty-two dollars in debt, told her casually one day that he had sold his vote for two dollars, Addams fell silent, unable to criticize his betrayal of democracy because she knew he had been tempted in ways she never had been.[21]

Addams and Starr had only been living in Hull House for a few months when they began to learn about the harsh realities of child labor. Several little girls refused the candy the two women offered them at Christmas because they had spent the last six weeks working fourteen-hour days in a candy factory and could not bear the taste or sight of it. In the neighborhood Addams and Starr found mothers and daughters at home sewing mounds of clothing for a few cents an hour. One four-year-old child pulled out basting threads hour after hour, sitting on a stool at her mother's feet.[22]

From these and many other stories and experiences, Addams learned that the poor were, on the whole, neither lazy nor immoral but simply trapped in a cycle of "toilsome and underpaid labor."[23] She met among them intelligent people of many talents and found herself forced to discard old assumptions about the stupidity of the poor. "It is a mistake," she pointed out, "to believe that all poor people are dull and lacking in intellectuality. People are poor because they have no ability to make money, but this may or may not be accompanied with ability in other directions."[24] The apparent "intellectual and moral superiority" of the upper classes, she concluded, rested on "economic props which are, after all, matters of accident."[25]

Hull House pursued practical solutions to the problems their neighbors faced. A day nursery and a kindergarten were opened in the first year, where, for a small fee, working mothers could place their pre-school children. To address the problems of low factory wages and cyclical unemployment in certain industries, Hull House encouraged workers to organize into unions and fight for better working conditions. To prevent the employment of young children, the House lobbied successfully for a new state law banning the practice.

Jane Addams preferred these types of solutions because they left her neighbors' dignity intact. Sometimes a gift of money, the usual form of charity, was necessary in an emergency, but she knew the more important gift was respect, because people prized it more highly than charity.[26] She felt that "contempt was the greatest crime one could commit against one's fellow man."[27] Determined not to condescend, she identified other motivations for her efforts, motivations that went beyond the usual ones of noblesse oblige and service.

A case in point was her views on the difficult subject of gratitude. Her wealthy friends like Louise deKoven Bowen viewed gratitude for their good work as the only payment they required of the poor. In this they felt noble. But Addams soon deflated them. In complaint one day Bowen told Addams, "I have done everything in the world for that woman and she is not even grateful." Bowen recalled that Jane Addams "looked at me quizzically and said, 'Is that the reason you helped her, because you wanted gratitude?'"[28] For Jane Addams, gratitude was not the point. She was helping them because they, like her, were part of the human race. This sense of fellowship left "no room for sensitiveness and gratitude."[29]

Addams's belief in "the solidarity of the human race" may have been inspired by literature and Christianity initially but life at Hull House deepened her understanding, as it also deepened the understanding of the other residents. One of them, Grace Abbott, learned on one occasion just what "solidarity" meant to Addams in practical terms.

An old Frenchman from the neighborhood was a chronic visitor to Hull House. He had, in his poverty and old age, been assigned by the county to the poorhouse in Oak Forest, a nearby suburb, but refused to go. Instead, he would regularly sit on the sofa in the Hull House reception room, "when and as it suited him," as Edith Abbott, another resident, described it. She felt that he should no longer be allowed to come to the crowded, busy room; his presence was a nuisance. She was also frustrated by his recalcitrance, since she sat on the charity district committee for Cook County that had assigned him to the poorhouse.

At Abbott's urging, Jane Addams politely asked the old man to go to the Infirmary, as the poorhouse was called, but he refused again. "Miss Addams," he said firmly, "it is a poorhouse. It is not a place for higher life." Addams, unwilling to evict him, let him remain, his dignity intact. He "continued to sit in our reception room," Abbott recalled, "as long as he was able to get there."[30]

One senses in Abbott's telling of the story that, at the time, she did not have the patience required to practice such respect, and that she knew it. She told the story many years later—an indication that she did not forget the lesson provided by Addams's example.

Through such experiences among the neighbors of Hull House, Addams and the other residents learned, as she had hoped, "from life itself," that "the things that make us alike are stronger and finer than the things that make us different. Human nature is essentially the same in a Chicago tenement or a Kansas farm."[31] Before moving to Hull House, Addams had imagined this was true. Now she knew it.

IV. The Humanity of the Wealthy

Jane Addams's views toward the wealthy were the same as her views toward the poor. The amount of money they controlled did not cause her to respect them more or less. Thus, although she regularly and effectively raised money for Hull House from her wealthy friends, she did not view them as being defined by their wealth. Emily Balch, a settlement and peace activist colleague of Addams, recalled that while Addams, "like the rest of us, liked some people and did not like others," she "never judged anyone as a member of any class or the bearer of any sort of label." Balch tells of "a wealthy woman [who was] very lonely because her family and old friends disliked her 'radical' interests while her labor friends seemed chiefly concerned with the money she could contribute. [She] told a friend, with tears in her eyes, that 'Miss Addams is interested in rich people too.'"[32]

As a wealthy person herself, Jane Addams was not intimidated by the wealth of others. This no doubt made it far easier for her to see them simply "as human beings." More remarkable was her ability to sympathize with them in their failings. She might have condemned them for lacking the fellow-feeling she believed in and practiced daily but there is no trace of anger in her writings regarding the wealthy as a class, only perplexity at their motives and sadness at their inability to break free.

One wealthy person she particularly studied was George Pullman, the millionaire owner of Pullman Car Company. He was one of the wealthiest men in Chicago, and, in his treatment of his striking workers, one of the cruelest. Deeply troubled by his actions, Addams pondered the reasons for his behavior in the months following the massive Pullman Strike. She decided that, while he had worked hard to be a generous benefactor to individuals in need, in her opinion, he gradually had lost "the power of attaining a simple human relationship with his employees," having forgotten "the common stock of experience which he held with his men."[33] "Successful struggle can often end," she wrote in another context, ". . . in a certain hardness of heart."[34]

Pullman shared with many other wealthy people a strong individualism and sense of being different. The rich, Addams knew from personal experience, tended not to have much group feeling. Indeed they had little ability to sympathize with people of their own class, let alone with those outside it. In one of her most remarkable essays, the "Introduction" to her first book, *Democracy and Social Ethics,* she pondered the reasons behind the short horizons of her well-read and well-traveled class.

People are not selfish, she decided, because they choose to be. Rather they are content to be ignorant. "We do not blame selfish people for [having] the will which chooses to be selfish," she wrote, "but for [having] the narrowness of interest which deliberately selects its experience within a limited sphere."[35] This has unfortunate consequences. Their judgments about society are impaired and their interest in broader society nil, except to the extent their own self-interest is at stake.

The solution was for people to mix "on the thronged and common road" of life, "where all must . . . at least see the size of another's burdens."[36] A broader set of experiences, she argued, would result in a "social perspective" and "sanity of judgment" that would be "the surest corrective of opinions concerning the social order and . . . efforts . . . for its improvement."[37] This would not only help them become more effective philanthropists; it would also bring meaning to their lives. Towards the end of this insightful essay, she put the challenge to her reader. "We are under a moral obligation," she wrote, "in choosing our experiences, since the result of those experiences must ultimately determine our understanding of life."[38]

Years earlier, during her second year at Hull House, she had put the same challenge even more directly to the women of her class who formed the membership of the Chicago Woman's Club. She told them in a talk, "We need the thrust in the side, the lateral pressure which comes from living next door to poverty."[39] She then reviewed the collective ground of their shared class lives, reminding them that "cultivation is self-destructive when shut away from human interests." With youthful brutal frankness, she noted that the "misdirected young life [of an upper-class young woman] seems to me as pitiful as the other great mass of destitute lives. . . . It is hard to tell which is most barren."[40] One wonders if a few of her audience did not squirm in their seats. This was perhaps not her most successful recruitment speech for Hull House. She was to learn soon enough how to couch her message in less stark terms.

By such speeches but primarily through personal contacts, she drew the wealthy and middle classes to Hull House. While some had had previous experience doing charity work with the poor, for others, as Kathleen McCarthy has noted, "the pungent sights and sounds of the West Side tenements were more foreign than the Egyptian bazaars and Parisian cafés which they visited with increasing regularity."[41] The lack of contact between the rich and poor so typical of the 1880s was a relatively new phenomenon. Before the Civil War, the rich had visited the poor with charity baskets and moral advice.[42] The settlement house movement, radical in its claim that social relations between rich and poor were a good thing, was, in its attempt to put the rich and poor back in touch with each other, a modern version of this older practice.

Beginning even before Hull House opened its doors, Addams had remarkable success in interesting and involving both the rich and the upper middle classes in the settlement and its neighborhood. An early friend was the architect Allen B. Pond, who helped her find the building that became Hull House and who was quick to embrace her philosophy that the rich could benefit from knowing the poor. In a church newsletter, Pond sought to spread the word: "Each of the lowest gets out of life, misery notwithstanding, something which he of the 'upper classes' has failed to discover," he wrote in 1890.[43] Pond, with his brother Irving, designed all of Hull House's buildings, while also serving as a trustee and secretary of Hull House Association from the board's founding in 1895 until his death in 1929. According to his brother, Allen's friendship with

Addams "greatly influenced the trend of [his] future activity outside his profession."[44] Allen Pond became a leading citizen of civic and social reform in Chicago, with a particular interest in low-income housing and municipal reform.

Another early wealthy friend of Hull House was William Kent, whom Jane Addams had first met in 1890, when he was a young man. A Yale graduate from a wealthy family, Mr. Kent had inherited from his father a block of tenement houses located across the street from Hull House that were as run down and neglected as any in the district. In a speech that was reported in the press, a Hull House resident took him to task for his heartlessness, with the happy result that he stopped by Hull House to defend himself and found himself, after talking with Jane Addams, turning over the tenements to Hull House to manage. That experiment failed, but, when the buildings were torn down and replaced with a new neighborhood playground, Mr. Kent and Hull House were equally pleased with the fruits of his philanthropy.[45]

Years later, however, what Kent most remembered and sought to record was what he had learned from Jane Addams about the poor. "The great difference in our points of view," he wrote, "was that Miss Addams had discovered and keenly realized that these people [his tenants] were human beings and filled in varying degrees with the same virtues and vices as other people. . . . She had learned that dirt was not . . . an article of faith [with the poor] but a by-product of poverty."[46] Kent became a volunteer at and a donor to Hull House, and served on the board of trustees. He applied the education he gained there in his subsequent careers as a Chicago politician and senator from California.

Among the wealthiest of Hull House's close friends was Louise deKoven Bowen. Daughter of a leading Chicago family and wife of a well-known businessman, Bowen was both rich and socially prominent. Serious-minded, she had been interested in charity work and helping the poor as a young mother, before she came to Hull House in 1896. Yet what she learned there was eye-opening: "My whole acquaintance with Hull House opened for me a new door into life. . . . I have made many good friends among working people and have come in contact with problems and situations about which I would have otherwise known nothing."[47]

Like Pond and Kent, Bowen was struck by the realization of the humanity she shared with the poor. "It was most interesting to realize," she recalled, "that although the people I met at Hull House lived a life far removed from the kind I led, yet, after all, we are all cast in the same mold, all with the same emotions, the same feelings, the same sense of right and wrong, but, alas, not with the same opportunities."[48]

Bowen came to believe firmly in the value of the settlement house's work, especially in its function as a bridge between the classes. "I began to feel that what was [most] needed . . . was an acquaintance between the well-to-do and those less well off. Until [this can happen], there will always be difficulties and there will never be that sympathy which should exist."[49] She was president of the Hull House Woman's Club for many years and a founder of the Juvenile Protection Association, which worked with the courts to address the special needs of youth defendants. She poured her wealth generously into Hull House, primarily to support her particular interests in boys and the Hull House Woman's Club. She financed two Hull House buildings, one for each group, and every year helped Jane Addams bail Hull House out of its annual debt. Like Pond's, her commitment to Hull House was whole-hearted and long-term. She joined the Hull House Association board in 1903 and served until 1944.[50] In her life, her understanding of the poor, and her philanthropy, Bowen pursued the pathway that was Addams's vision. Bowen did not allow her wealth to prevent her from following Jane Addams's admonishment to "hook yourself fast with your whole mind to [the] neighborhood."[51]

Addams's wealthy friends were enthusiastic capitalists. Their experience at Hull House did not change this, but, motivated by their growing realization that the poor were victims of a harsh environment, several of them found themselves viewing corporations' treatment of their employees in a new light. Indeed, in cases where they themselves owned stock in a company that was mistreating its employees, they began to feel partially responsible for the grievances of which they were now learning. Bowen, who learned of the dangerous working conditions at the Pullman Company from Hull House resident Alice Hamilton in 1911, felt compelled as a major stockholder to write the company's president and ask him to review the situation and meet with her to discuss solutions. Eventually she succeeded in prompting the company to make the needed improvements. She undertook a similar effort with International Harvester, persuading that company to cease employing women all night and to provide women with a living minimum wage.[52]

The principle that the corporations had an ethical responsibility to treat their employees well was also applied in reverse. Like other social reformers of the day, Jane Addams and her Hull House friends believed that a corporation that treated its employees badly should not be permitted to assuage its conscience by making gifts to Hull House to benefit those same employees. This was the concept of "tainted money."

When such a situation arose, it provided a Hull House trustee, major donor and businessman William Colvin, with an education. He had found a factory owner who was willing to give $20,000 to support the construction of a new building on Hull House land for the Jane Club, a cooperative housing club for working girls. But when Mr. Colvin brought back the news of the gift and revealed to the residents the name of the donor, he was soon informed of the man's cruel employment practices. He came to see that, as Jane Addams described it, "it would be impossible to erect a clubhouse for working girls with such money." Persuaded of this new way of looking at things, Mr. Colvin, with some embarrassment, had to tell the factory owner that he must now refuse the gift he had just solicited from him.[53]

The lesson Colvin learned was not unanticipated. Addams often warned people not to be alarmed if they found their ethical standards broadening as they became acquainted with the real facts of the lives of their neighbors.[54] This, too, was part of what Hull House was all about.

V. The Benefits to the Philanthropist

Most of Hull House's major donors were active volunteers in one or more Hull House activities; as a result, their volunteer work shaped, informed, and fueled their philanthropy. Not surprisingly, their monetary gifts to Hull House reflected the wisdom they had gained: the typical Hull House project was designed as much as possible to address the root causes of problems, rather than treat short-term symptoms.[55]

Addams viewed this grounding in reality as essential to effective philanthropy. She wrote, "A man who takes the betterment of humanity for his aim and end must also take the daily experiences of humanity for the constant correction of his process. He must . . . test and guide his achievement by human experience."[56]

By such knowledge the donor could avoid the twin pitfalls of "indiscriminate giving," on the one hand, and "the stern policy of withholding" on the other. The first occurs, she wrote, when the donor, viewing matters from a distance, is filled with mercy; giving motivated solely by kindness "has disastrous results." The second comes from a single-minded commitment to justice, again when the donor is viewing matters from a distance, and produces in the donor a "dreary lack of sympathy and an understanding that the establishment of justice is impossible." Recalling the biblical injunction to love mercy and to do justly, she concluded, "It may be that the combination of the two can never be attained save as we fulfill the third requirement—'to walk humbly with God,'" which to her meant "to walk for many dreary miles . . . in the company of the humble."

As a long-time resident of Hull House, she did not romanticize the experience. She knew it would offer not "peace of mind" but "the pangs and throes to which the poor human understanding is subjected whenever it attempts to comprehend the meaning of life."[57] Part of the pain came from the new self-knowledge philanthropists would gain—self-knowledge that was vital to their effectiveness.

Addams believed that they could only succeed if they could recognize in themselves the humanity they saw in the poor. The philanthropist, she wrote, "must succeed or fail in proportion as he has incorporated that experience [of humanity] with his own [human experience]." If he does not, conceit and arrogance follow. "His own achievements," she wrote, "become his stumbling block, and he comes to believe in his own goodness as something outside himself. He makes an exception of himself, and thinks that he is different from the rank and file of his fellows."[58]

Jane Addams often spoke of the transformational power of the first-hand knowledge of the lives of the poor that her friends were gaining. Ever the philosopher, she liked to describe the process abstractly. "We are under a moral obligation in choosing our experiences, since the results of those experiences must ultimately determine our understanding of life." But the advantages went beyond understanding; they included redemption, both for the individual and society. "The subjective necessity for social settlements," she wrote, "is identical with that necessity which urges us toward social and individual salvation."[59]

Although she inherited wealth, Jane Addams did not, after some struggle, permit her wealth to dominate her life. She chose instead to travel the "thronged and common" road that she came to believe every person should travel, where people could "see each other's burdens" and discover what they shared as human beings.[60]

She believed that the individual who sought such experience would benefit and so would society. Like many before and after her, from Plato to Robert Bellah, Addams held that there was an intimate relationship between the moral character of a people and the nature of its political and social community. The exploration of the meaning of life was, among other things, a civic responsibility.

In her view, to undertake such an exploration, not to dispense their wealth properly, was the important task facing the rich, or, indeed, any human being. The responsibilities of the wealthy were the responsibilities of the poor: to be active, involved members of the human community. She did not discount the power of money but she knew its limits, having explored them as a young woman. "We forget," she wrote, "that capital cannot enter the moral realm."[61] Like Ruskin, she held that "there is no wealth but life," that life is the most important wealth that humanity has to share.[62]

Today's philanthropists have much to gain from considering Addams's views on the "responsibilities of being human." Too often we of the wealthy and the middle classes have no contact with the people whom we support with our philanthropy, preferring simply to send our checks across town. Or, if we volunteer, it is only to raise money from others of our class, not to participate in the programs that serve the working poor, the unemployed, and the dropouts. Ignorant of how hard the poor work and the extent to which their lives are shaped by forces beyond their control, we too quickly condemn them for their lack of work ethic and self-discipline and for their failure to climb out of poverty.

Disrespecting and distrustful of the poor, we design our philanthropy accordingly. The policies of the states and the federal government toward the poor, those policies representing a major arm of modern philanthropy, reflect our biases. Exhortation, social science research, and dramatic news stories have made little dent in the class assumptions of the voters. True welfare reform remains politically out of reach.

Cross-class social relations may be part of the answer. Although the idea sounds Victorian, it needn't. One is cheered to note that Morton M. Kondrake of *The New Republic* recently suggested it. He wrote, "If there is ever to be a consensus again [in the United States] behind efforts to help the poor, it will have to come—or at least is most likely to come—from sustained human contact between middle-class voters (and rich people too) and individual poor."[63]

Today cross-class relations are as elusive as ever. Most of us in the middle and upper classes live and work in what Robert N. Bellah and his colleagues have termed "life style enclaves." Like Addams, we are isolated in our class. Still, like her, we can escape through our volunteer work.[64] We can follow our gifts of money across town, to the charities of our choice. For the sake of both the country and ourselves, more of us need to travel the "thronged and common road."

Notes

1. Jane Addams, *Twenty Years at Hull House with Autobiographical Notes* (New York: Macmillan Company, 1910), p. 123.

2. Jane Addams, "A Book That Changed My Life," *Christian Century* 44 (October 13, 1927), p. 1196.

3. Benjamin Disraeli, *Sybil, or Two Nations* (New York: Thomas Nelson and Sons, 1940), p. 85.

4. Jane Addams, "A Function of the Social Settlement," *Annals of the American Academy* 13 (May 1899): 33.

5. Addams, *Twenty Years*, p. 73.

6. Ibid., p. 17.

7. George Eliot, *Adam Bede* (New York: Viking Penguin, 1986), p. 229. In her unpublished speech, "Outgrowths of Toynbee Hall," delivered in December 1890, Addams acknowledges Eliot as a passionate advocate for humanity (p. 8). Jane Addams Peach Collection, Swarthmore College.

8. Ralph Waldo Emerson, "Man the Reformer," in *America's Voluntary*

Spirit, A Book of Readings, ed. Brian O'Connell (New York: The Foundation Center, 1983), p. 51.

9. Addams, *Twenty Years,* p. 77.

10. Jane Addams, "Outgrowths of Toynbee Hall," p. 8. Jane Addams's religious motivations were initially and remained far more central to her work than has been generally recognized. But that is a topic for another essay.

11. Addams, *Twenty Years,* p. 117.

12. Addams, "Outgrowths," p. 4.

13. Addams, *Twenty Years,* p. 85.

14. Ibid., p. 88.

15. Addams, "Outgrowths," p. 13.

16. Ellen Starr to Mary Blaisdell, February 23, 1889, Star Papers. Sophia Smith Collection. Smith College, Northampton, Mass.

17. Jane Addams, "The Subjective Necessity for Social Settlements," *Philanthropy and Social Progress,* ed. Henry C. Addams (New York: Thomas Y. Crowell & Co., 1893), p. 1.

18. Jane Addams, "Hull House as a Type of College Settlement," *Proceedings, Wisconsin State Conference of Charities and Corrections* (1894), p. 97.

19. Several of her colleagues in the settlement house movement recalled observing her listening to her neighbors throughout the 1890s. When Graham Taylor, who founded the Chicago Commons Settlement, first began visiting Hull House in 1893, he wrote (Graham Taylor, "Jane Addams: The Great Neighbor," *Survey Graphic* 24 [July 1935]) that he "almost always found her listening" to one or more of her neighbors (p. 338). Mary Simkovitch, who founded the Greenwich House Settlement in New York City, described (Mary Simkovitch, *Memorial Service for Jane Addams* [National Conference of Social Work Memorial Service: June 1935]) her as "always in that listening attitude of mind of 'what is it?'" (p. 6).

20. Addams, *Twenty Years,* p. 168.

21. Jane Addams, "Ethical Survivals in Municipal Corruption," *International Journal of Ethics* VIII (April 1898), p. 284.

22. Addams, *Twenty Years,* p. 198.

23. Addams, "Outgrowths," p. 11.

24. Jane Addams, "The Settlement," *Proceedings of the Illinois Conference of Charities* (1896), p. 57.

25. Addams, "A Function," p. 32.

26. Lillian Wald, paraphrasing Jane Addams in "Afterword" to *Forty Years at Hull House* by Jane Addams (New York: The Macmillan Company, 1935), p. 432.

27. Alice Hamilton, *Exploring the Dangerous Trades* (1943; repr., Boston: Northeastern University Press, 1985), p. 59.

28. Louise deKoven Bowen, *Growing Up with a City* (New York: Macmillan Company, 1926), p. 87.

29. Jane Addams, *Democracy and Social Ethics* (New York: Macmillan, 1902), p. 154.

30. Edith Abbott, "Hull House Years," a chapter in an unpublished biography of Grace Abbott by Edith Abbott. Grace and Edith Abbott Papers, p. 29; Special Collections, Regenstein Library. University of Chicago.

31. Addams, "The Settlement," p. 58.

32. Emily Greene Balch, *Beyond Nationalism: The Social Thought of Emily Greene Balch,* ed. Mercedes M. Randall (New York: Twayne Publishers, 1972), p. 206.

33. Jane Addams, "A Modern Lear," in *The Social Thought of Jane Addams,* ed. Christopher Lasch (New York: The Bobbs-Merrill Company, 1965), p. 112.

34. Jane Addams, "Municipal Administration," *The American Journal of Sociology* X (January 1905), p. 444.

35. Addams, *Democracy,* p. 10.

36. Ibid., p. 6

37. Ibid., p. 7.

38. Ibid., p. 9.

39. Addams, "Outgrowths," p. 3.

40. Ibid., p. 6.

41. Kathleen D. McCarthy, *Noblesse Oblige: Charity and Cultural Philanthropy in Chicago, 1849–1929* (Chicago: The University of Chicago Press, 1982), p. 31.

42. Ibid., p.18.

43. Scrapbook I, p. 5. Jane Addams Memorial Collection. University of Illinois at Chicago Library. University of Illinois at Chicago.

44. Irving Pond, chapter 7, ms. autobiography, p. E-17. The Irving Pond papers. Archives, American Academy of Arts and Sciences, New York.

45. Addams, *Twenty Years,* pp. 289–291.

46. William Kent, "Jane Addams," pp. 13–14. The William Kent Family Papers. Yale University Library, Yale University.

47. Bowen, *City,* p. 92.

48. Ibid., p. 94.

49. Ibid., p. 93.

50. *Notable American Women, The Modern Period,* s.v. "Louise deKoven Bowen."

51. Addams, "Hull House as a Type of College Settlement," p. 97.

52. Bowen, *City,* pp. 165–166; Louise deKoven Bowen, *Speeches, Addresses and Letters of Louise deKoven Bowen, Reflecting Social Movement in Chicago* (Ann Arbor, Mich.: Edwards Brothers, Inc., 1937) ed. Mary E. Humphrey, I, p. 168.

53. Addams, *Twenty Years,* p. 138.

54. H. F. Hegner, "Scientific Value of the Social Settlements," *American Journal of Sociology* III (September 1897), p. 176.

55. Addams, *Democracy,* p. 9.

56. Ibid., p. 176.

57. Ibid., p. 70.

58. Ibid.

59. Addams, "Subjective Necessity," p. 26.

60. Ibid., p. 6.

61. Jane Addams, *The Excellent Becomes the Permanent* (New York: Macmillan, 1932), p. 45.

62. John Ruskin, *Unto This Last* (New York: Crowell & Co., 1872), p. 125.

63. Morton M. Kondrake, "Just Say Yes," *The New Republic* 200 (April 24, 1989), p. 12.

64. Robert N. Bellah; Richard Madsen; William M. Sullivan; Ann Swidler; and Steven M. Tipton, *Habits of the Heart: Individualism and Commitment in American Life* (New York: Harper & Row, 1985), p. 75.

God *and* Money

ROBERT L. PAYTON

Part of the mission of a comprehensive center is to span the whole field of philanthropy and the whole scope of the university; teaching, research, and service. Two areas that the Indiana University Center is building in depth are fund raising and ethics and values. It is the deep tension between fund raising realities and ethical and religious values that seems to me most interesting. If we embrace both of those perspectives we will have embraced the matrix of the spiritual and the material, of the religious and the economic, of the ethical aspirations and the practical techniques that are the defining characteristics of philanthropy. Therefore, my short essay on "God and Money" is intended to compress both perspectives into as tight a conceptual space as possible.

And so I approach the subject of religion and philanthropy as one of those concerned with finding ways to study and teach the subject. There is another reason for attending carefully to religion and philanthropy. It is embedded in the research undertaken by Independent Sector and a few others into the giving and volunteering behavior of Americans. For me, the most important information coming out of the research thus far has to do with the behavior of those people who place a high value on religion and who express that value by attending church regularly and frequently. The recent (1988) Independent Sector report on its national survey of Giving and Volunteering contains this information:[1]

Average annual household giving is $562; average giving among

Based on a paper presented at the Independent Sector Research Forum, March 12, 1989.

those who attend church weekly is $1,109. The average percentage of giving for all givers is 1.5 percent of household income; among those who attend church weekly the average is 2.7 percent. The average number of hours volunteered per week is 2.1; the average number of hours volunteered per week by those who attend church frequently is 3.2. The number of people who attend church weekly is 29 percent of the total; those who rarely or never attend represent 32 percent of the total.

I draw some rough inferences from these and other even more familiar figures. Philanthropic giving and volunteering is dominated by those most actively involved in organized religion. No other field of activity claims even a third as many of the philanthropic dollars contributed as does religion. Of even more notable interest is that giving to religion is the means by which many Americans support other nonreligious organizations and causes.

My own working conclusion is that the strength of American philanthropy is based upon its religious origins and values and traditions. My own conviction—and it must be merely that, because I can't prove it—is that philanthropy would not survive the significant deterioration of its religious values and character. I am not arguing that all philanthropy is religious; I am arguing that the American philanthropic tradition is religious, in its philanthropic as well as in its charitable dimension. The theory of philanthropy is built upon the reality of charity, as much for the nonreligious Carnegie as for the believing Rockefeller, as much for the secular Sierra Club as for the religious Salvation Army.

The anthropologist Mary Douglas once commented to me that one doesn't need religion to explain the origins of philanthropy. A similar perspective is shared by some historians, and probably by many if not most social scientists. Many who approach religion from the perspective of other disciplines explain religious behavior in nonreligious terms. I am not yet persuaded that these others' views are more enlightening, but I am convinced that the diverse perspectives add up to an issue worth examining more carefully and discussing more fully.

There is a third inference that I've drawn from the first two: If people who attend church weekly lead the way in giving and volunteering, and if there is a close link between their behavior and

their religious commitments, then it seems to me very important
that we should know more about these people if we hope to understand American philanthropy as it now exists.

Not being a disciplined scholar I draw readily on my experience
to test what I think I know. My experience includes involvement
at varying levels of activity over the years in two mainline Protestant
denominations. My reading and observation and some of my involvement with those denominations has been at the level of the
denomination as well as at the level of the congregation. I have
known some members of the clergy as close personal friends, others
as intellectual and professional colleagues. And I have sat in the
pews with other lay people like myself. I don't recommend that
others follow my approach, and I hope that more rigorous inquiry
buttresses our knowledge of philanthropy as an element of congregational life.

Serious understanding of American philanthropy is not often to
be found at the denominational level. It is rarely found among the
clergy or among those who teach the clergy in theological schools.
In my opinion the denominational leadership is philanthropically
out of touch with the people in the pews. It has become preoccupied
with issues at the national and international level to an extent that
simply passes beyond the interest among ordinary churchgoers. It
seems obvious that at the denominational level it has been politics
rather than philanthropy that church leaders are most interested
in. Some seem clearly to share the view that voluntary action is a
poor substitute for governmental action. Efforts to increase voluntary giving and voluntary service are seen as an obstruction to
social progress.

My purpose is not to dismiss as unimportant the issues that the
denominations urge upon us. The struggle over the social gospel
is at least a century old and the debate is as important now as it
was then. My sense is that religious understanding rises up from
immediate experience. The links between that understanding
among parishioners and the grand social conceptualizing of the
denominational leaders are not strong enough to support the programs that are advocated. The resulting sense is one of continually
falling short at the larger levels of ambition—when there is in fact
much to be praised and admired at the local level. Irving Kristol

told a relevant story at the national meeting of the Council on Foundations a few years ago:

> I'll never forget my first job, working for a fine mechanic, who was an illiterate and who owned the factory. After I'd been there a few days, he took me aside and said, "Irving, I want you to remember two things; First, a thing worth doing is worth doing cheaply. And second, if something is too hard to do, find something easier to do."[2]

The most obvious difference between the denominational and the congregational level is that congregations do what is doable.

My friends in the clergy remind me of many of my academic colleagues. They look upon fund raising with distaste. Some of them act as if money comes into the university at night. The essential obstacle may be that of self-esteem: if I am a worthy scholar, as I know I am, others will know that and make it possible for me to do my work. A more recent variant is that as a scholar I have rights to do scholarship; therefore, I have a claim on the public treasury.

The clergy are often bogged down in Washington Gladden's worries about "tainted money." At times they are quite understandably concerned that they can't give their whole commitment to the people they serve if they must turn to the same people for financial support. The larger questions of stewardship and trusteeship are often submerged in what becomes a dreary burden of annual pledge appeals. The members of the congregation can rotate their responsibilities for stewardship; the pastor cannot.

When I think of the people in the pews I conclude that that is where the backbone of American philanthropy rests. They are effective for several reasons.

The first reason is that people who attend church regularly are educated into the tradition of serving others. They are reminded of it every week. They are called upon to give their time and their money to serve others. They are told that that is what religion is all about, reducing all of it to loving God above all and loving one's neighbor as oneself.

The second reason is that the American tradition of philanthropy, shaped as much as it has been by the Protestant tradition, assumes that each person should be immediately involved in voluntary giving and voluntary service. The people who attend church regularly appear to be active people, as well—even attending church every week is a sign of self-discipline and sustained motivation. Such people are concerned about their neighbors, and so much of their philanthropy is "informal"—they are engaged in philanthropic activity on a level that is often loosely organized or not organized at all. (One of the great limitations of our way of talking about organized philanthropy is that it ignores this pervasive and powerful informal kind.)

The third reason why the people in the pews are so important is that they believe in the principle of self-help and the principle of mutual aid as well as in the principle of philanthropy. They recognize the range of action that is called for and they can appreciate the differences.

The fourth reason is that these people (a) believe in God, and (b) practice pragmatism. Whatever theological debates are going on in the pulpit or at the national conferences, the people in the pews are the ones charged with getting things done. And they do everything: not only do they raise the money to pay the pastor and maintain the church property and to help the homeless, they attend to all of the other ordinary problems of buying and arranging the flowers on the altar and then, after the service, taking those flowers to people in the hospital. The mockery of these bourgeois virtues by modern intellectuals is so common that we rarely react to it anymore. The fact is that morality is always grounded in the ordinary behavior of ordinary people, and these ordinary religious people see it as their work to do some of the good that needs to be done in the world. Pious as they may be on Sunday, most of them are involved on every other day in useful philanthropic work.

If American philanthropy has a philosophy, I think we will find it in American pragmatism. We should look for the truth of philanthropy in the behavior of ordinary people engaged in the routine work of life.

The fifth reason why the people in the pews are so important is that they are more than religious in their values and interests and activities. One evening I attended the annual business meeting of a reasonably large and active congregation. In addition to church matters, members in attendance reported on other activities: the hospital fund raising campaign; the new organization of parents and teachers and community leaders to deal with alcohol and drug abuse among teenagers, housing for a family moving into the area from South Africa; Amnesty International letter writing; and several musical and dramatic performances.

All of these things involved members of the congregation not simply as religious believers but as members of the community. Because this took place in a Long Island suburban church, many of those present were also active in business and governmental organizations and educational institutions in New York City and elsewhere in the metropolitan area. People who attend church weekly contribute their time and money not only to their church but to a wide array of other so-called secular purposes. There is a longstanding close working relationship between church-going business people and churches in doing all sorts of community work. Their cooperation is seen in the orchestration of efforts in the United Way and other community organizations.

If this general view of how much of the power of American philanthropy is among those anonymous people in the congregations has any merit, where does it lead? One direction is toward the education of the denominational leadership and the clergy about the reality of philanthropy. A second and perhaps more important direction is toward the fuller education of the laity about how they can do more than they are already doing. Many of us know individuals of substantial means and few commitments who don't know how to go about donating their wealth for philanthropic purposes. "Planned giving" remains a mystery to most Americans of means. That ignorance extends to many of the professionals in finance, accounting, law, and tax work.

The educational effort within the churches must also address the weakness of so much giving and fund raising for religious purposes. The powerful appeals to emotion and crisis overemphasize the immediate and neglect the long term. They imply quick solutions to intractable problems. Such approaches do not lead people to long term commitment but to a continuing, dizzying series of emergencies. Many people manage to maintain their equilibrium but others become confused. The most difficult tension within philanthropy is the tension between the immediate and the long term. Religious education in philanthropy has developed commitment and even generosity for the immediate, but not understanding for the future.

A third course to follow recognizes that the goal of expanding giving among those whose religious values are strong is not simply to increase giving to religion. The churches can become much more effective facilitators for giving for all sorts of purposes. What must happen is that the networks represented in each congregation must be mobilized to become more effective.

The longer term goal, of course, is to expand the numbers of people who give generously of their time as well as their money. The link between the two kinds of voluntary action is essential if philanthropy is going to avoid the trap of throwing money at problems. One of the principles of effective philanthropy has always been to be close to the recipient; that happens best and most often at the level of community. In the religious tradition, this means at the level of the congregation.

A final observation: the surveys would lead us to conclude that people who are wealthier than the average and better educated than the average attend church less often. The research does not yet bring it out, but I suspect that it is because the means and the knowledge of the wealthy and the educated give them a sense of mastery over their lives. They tend to be "youthful" in outlook in one very important way—they think themselves invulnerable. People who attend church regularly sense their vulnerability, perhaps because they are closer to it, more exposed to it every day. The ones in church know they are vulnerable, and that everyone is. That is why philanthropy makes so much sense in religion, and why religion is so important to philanthropy.

Notes

1. Independent Sector: "Giving and Volunteering in the United States: Findings from a National Survey," Washington, D.C., 1988.

2. Irving Kristol, "Foundations and the Sin of Pride: The Myth of the 'Third Sector,'" The Institute for Educational Affairs, Washington, D.C., 1980. (Remarks at the annual conference of the Council on Foundations, Houston, May 30, 1980.)

contributors

ALBERT ANDERSON is a principal in the private consulting firm of Anderson/Swenson. A former teacher of philosophy and administrator, he has most recently served as Vice President for Planning/Administration at the University of Minnesota Foundation.

DWIGHT F. BURLINGAME is the Associate Director for Academic Programs and Research at the Indiana University Center on Philanthropy. He is a frequent speaker, consultant, and author on topics relating to philanthropy, libraries, and development.

KENNETH FOX is a research consultant in urban economic development and planning. His most recent book is *Metropolitan America: Urban Life and Urban Policy in the United States, 1940–1980.*

BARRY D. KARL is the Norman and Edna Freehling Professor of History at the University of Chicago. He is the author of *The Uneasy State: The United States from 1915 to 1945* and *Charles E. Merriam and the Study of Politics.*

LOUISE W. KNIGHT, Director of Development at United South End Settlements in Boston, Massachusetts, is writing a biography of Jane Addams.

ROBERT L. PAYTON is Director of the Center on Philanthropy and Professor of Philanthropic Studies at Indiana University/Purdue University at Indianapolis. Among his many writings in philanthropy and education is *Philanthropy: Voluntary Action for the Public Good.*

JONATHAN RILEY, Associate Professor in both the Department of Political Science and Murphy Institute of Political Economy at Tulane University, is the author of *Liberal Utilitarianism* and *Liberty in Private Matters: Mill's Classic Doctrine.*